TECHNIQUES
of
UPHOLSTERY

**Easy Chairs, Settees
and
Occasional Chairs**

by
Robert James McDonald

B.T. Batsford Ltd, London

© Robert James McDonald 1987
First published 1987

ISBN 0 7134 5631 0

Printed in Great Britain by
R J Acford Ltd
Chichester, Sussex
for the publishers
B T Batsford Ltd
4 Fitzhardinge Street
London W1H 0AH

Contents

Introduction

This is the second in a series of four books taking the craft of upholstery several stages further than the work I described in Book 1. Projects included in this book are more difficult and challenging because they are larger and more complicated. However, I have included text which is easy to read and understand and instructions with many simple line drawings and photographs.

My purpose with this series is to give you, the reader, a closer and more detailed coverage of specific projects in a graded system throughout the four books. You would therefore be able to select one book which could carry details of the particular type of upholstery that you want to specialize in.

Projects dealt with in Book 1 are mostly for smaller items of upholstery that can be worked upon on a small table or worktop with little upset to the rest of the household. The larger items featured in this book, however, will need a clear working space and probably cause a certain amount of débris and dust. If you intend to carry out the work at home, lay a dust cover or sheet over the floor. This will protect the surface from the old tacks that you rip out of the work and become embedded in the floor or carpet. The old tacks, which are unusable, should be gathered up from time to time and disposed of.

To avoid many hours of unnecessary back aches and pain, where possible, raise the item, whether it is a chair or

1. Trestle suitable for upholstery work

settee, and place it at a comfortable working height. You can carry out work much more comfortably by doing this.

Figure 1 shows a trestle which professionals use for standing upholstery on when working. Should you intend to carry out much upholstery, a pair of trestles would be an excellent investment. You can make them from soft or hard wood.

Like most craft work, upholstering requires a degree of skill which will improve with practice, and above all, demands your patience. It is unwise to undertake a project which is too ambitious, without first trying a simpler item to give you the feel of the soft and flexible materials and the confidence to handle them. I have also noticed that women often enjoy upholstery more than men do because, unless they have been trained in the craft, men find working with wood and metal easier than fabric.

As mentioned earlier, patience is an important virtue when learning upholstery techniques. It is very tempting to finish a job quickly without properly considering the final appearance, smooth line, and sculptured look of the work.

To obtain the professional look, ample temporary tacking at all times is needed. A professional upholsterer will always 'temporary' tack inner materials and outer covering before finally 'tacking off'. This term is one that I will use frequently throughout the book.

To temporary tack, align the material being worked on as straight as possible and hammer tacks to hold the material onto the timber so that the tacks are only partly into their depth. After temporary tacking on all sides, inspect the work and check the straightness of weave lines, tensions of material and flowing lines of work. If any of these are not satisfactory at the temporary tacking stage you can simply lift the tacks out and reposition or re-align them to satisfaction. Rarely can you lay a piece of material onto an upholstered surface, tack 'home', and find that the straightness or line is perfect. Temporary tacking ensures against bad workmanship — it should never be omitted.

MATERIALS

A problem which many amateurs undertaking upholstery frequently find most difficult, other than the work itself, is locating a supplier of upholstery materials. This is not as difficult with modern upholstery when you are perhaps replacing resilient rubber webbing or renewing foam cushions or foam filling as most of these commodities can be purchased at the larger D.I.Y. stores or even local smaller traders.

Other types of supplies that may be used for refurbishing a traditionally upholstered piece are rather more difficult to track down. You may need linen or jute webbing, hessian (canvas), different sizes and gauges of coil springs, fillings such as fibre and horsehair, and a variety of other bits and pieces including tacks of different sizes.

To help you with the problem of finding supplies, the appendix includes a useful list of addresses of suppliers of upholstery sundries spread throughout the country. These traders should be able to supply the enthusiastic amateur with most items in small amounts. Unfortunately, wholesale suppliers to the upholstery manufacturers will not sell the items on a small scale.

TACKS AND STAPLES

Using tacks or wire staples for fixing upholstering materials to the timber frame is optional. Staples fired into the material and frame using a compressed air tool are widely used by today's manufacturers producing modern styles of upholstery with the use of modern materials. This method speeds up production and is less costly than using steel tacks. The home-based upholstery worker, of course, would not have the benefit of compressed air or of such a staple-firing tool, but there are some reliable and strong manual staple-firing tools on the market which are easily obtainable. Figure 2 shows such a tool in use.

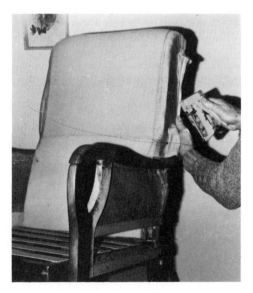

2. Using hand stapling tool

Suitable sizes of staples to use with these tools are 6 mm ($\frac{1}{4}$ in) and 8 mm ($\frac{5}{16}$ in). This measurement refers to the length of the leg of the staple; widths of staples are normally 12–13 mm ($\frac{1}{2}$ in). The normal paper-fixing staples are too soft for upholstery as considerable pressure is required to force the wire staple into the hard wood frame. A good staple-firing tool is an asset for the person about to embark on a series of upholstery projects using modern materials.

Temporary fixing materials is still as necessary when you use a staple-firing tool as when you use tacks. To do this hold the stapling tool a little distance away from the fixing point as the staple is fired into the timber. The staple will penetrate the timber only partly, enabling you to remove it easily with pliers or a small screwdriver when you adjust the material.

Staples, however, should not be used for fixing materials on certain kinds of upholstery work – that is, most traditional forms of upholstery, particularly the refurbishing of antique upholstery. Linen webbing, hessian (canvas), calico, leather etc. usually requires a traditional tack for a sound, lasting job.

Normally the professional upholsterer using the tacking method would have a range of tacks to hand, conveniently stored in small hanging bags close to his work.

The range of tacks available for upholstery is: 16 mm ($\frac{5}{8}$ in); 13 mm ($\frac{1}{2}$ in); and 10 mm ($\frac{3}{8}$ in). There are larger and smaller tacks available but the home upholsterer would probably not need them. In addition, each size is produced in 'improved' and 'fine' forms. The term improved describes a tack with a thicker shank and a larger width of head than its fine counterpart, seen in figure 3. With the wide selection of materials to be tacked during upholstering some are best tacked with the improved tack: for example, use 16 mm ($\frac{5}{8}$ in) improved tacks on woven webbing or hessian and scrim (loosely woven materials) on the thick timber of the underframe on an easy chair or settee; use 13 mm ($\frac{1}{2}$ in) improved tacks for webbing and hessian on lighter timber and 13 mm ($\frac{1}{2}$ in) fine for resilient rubber webbing. Use

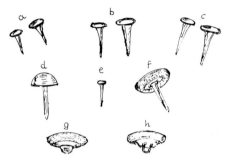

3. **a** 10 mm ($\frac{3}{8}$ in) fine and improved tacks **b** 13 mm ($\frac{1}{2}$ in) fine and improved tacks **c** 16 mm ($\frac{5}{8}$ in) fine and improved tacks **d** oxidised decorative nail **e** gimp pin **f** covered stud **g** covered button with tuft **h** covered button with wire loop

10 mm ($\frac{3}{8}$ in) tacks for calico or coverings on polished rebated edges.

The basic principle in selecting the appropriate tack for a particular operation is to choose the smallest size which will successfully hold the material sufficiently strongly and also the size of tack which will not split the timber, particularly on the lighter frames. For the amateur upholsterer probably 16 mm ($\frac{5}{8}$ in) improved would suffice for webbing heavy work and 13 mm ($\frac{1}{2}$ in) or 10 mm ($\frac{3}{8}$ in) for fine work.

In addition to tacks, 'gimp' pins are very useful for certain operations. These are very slender tacks with very small heads and available in black lacquer or other colours. These are extremely convenient for holding covering or fixing gimp into position. Use the appropriate colour to blend with the colour of the covering or gimp, and make them practically invisible by easing up one or two threads alongside the gimp pin and laying them over the head of the pin.

Tacks are available from most D.I.Y. stores, although purchasing them in small packs does work out expensive; they can be purchased in larger quantities of 500 g (1lb 2oz) or more at upholstery shops.

TOOLS

Figure 4 shows tools normally used by the traditional up-holsterer. Each one of the tools illustrated is not vitally necessary for the home upholsterer. Substitute tools often may be found and used successfully but if you plan to do a good deal of upholstery the correct tools would be a good investment.

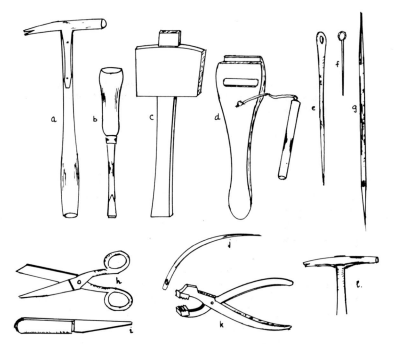

4. Upholstery tools: **a** upholsterer's hammer **b** ripping chisel **c** mallet **d** webbing stretcher **e** regulator **f** skewers **g** bayonet needle **h** scissors **i** leather knife **j** spring needle **k** hide strainer **l** cabriole hammer

5. Use of a piece of wood to tension linen webbing

Figure 5 illustrates how you can tension woven linen or jute webbing using a piece of wood instead of the traditional upholsterer's webbing stretching tool. A light weight cabinet maker's hammer with small face may substitute for the upholsterer's hammer; an old screwdriver may be used to remove tacks in conjunction with a hammer with a large face instead of the conventional ripping chisel and mallet as illustrated. Do not use a new or good screwdriver for this tack-removing operation if using it with a hammer, as the wooden handle will quickly be damaged; always use a wood mallet against any wooden handled tool. A large circular needle, usually available at drapery stores, could replace a spring needle.

Unfortunately, there is no substitute for the long upholsterer's stitching needle used for 'blind' stitching, rolls and stitched edges, but normally these should be fairly easy to obtain and not too expensive.

STRIPPING UPHOLSTERY

Frequently, it is necessary to re-cover only an item of upholstery without any major repair to the actual interior. The method of re-covering varies a great deal depending upon the type of upholstery in question. If, for example, the item has foam filling as in figure 2 this is easily removed without too much bother. Covering on upholstery such as this is generally held in place with staples; these may be difficult to remove if a compressed air tool has been used to insert them. Remove as many staples as possible whilst stripping the covering. Ease them out with a narrow-blade screwdriver or other pointed tool – an upholsterer's regulator, if available, is ideal, being thin, pointed and strong. Force the point of the tool under the crown of the staple, lifting the staple from the covering and finally lifting them out with pliers. If it is impossible to lift the staple out of the timber, snip the covering alongside with a sharp knife or scissors to pull the covering away.

A word of safety – whilst using a pointed tool, do not hold the item with your hand behind the staple being removed as the tool may slip and injure you.

Stripping traditionally upholstered items needs a little more thought and a systematic approach as generally each part will be fixed with tacks. If the upholstery has been stuffed and stitched with horsehair or fibre you may find that sections of the stuffing have been fixed into position over a piece of covering which had been positioned during an earlier stage in the upholstering. In this case, the covering will need to be cut away if complete removal of the stuffing is not intended. The easiest and most convenient method of stripping covering from an easy chair or settee is by working systematically on one section at a time. Firstly, upturn the item, resting the seat upon a stool, chair seat or box (*figure* 6). This will put it at a suitable height to help you remove tacks or staples holding the bottoming fabric and base edges of the outer covering — that is, outside back, outside arms and border.

At all times hammer tacks out using the ripping tool

or screwdriver in the direction of the grain of the timber (*figure* 6). Forcing tacks out against the grain or across the width of the rail may cause pieces of timber to break away or split a rail close to its joint, thus giving additional work in repairs to the frame.

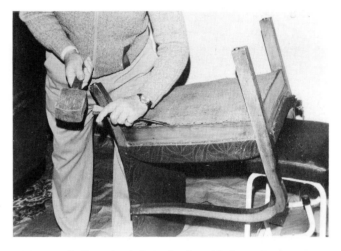

6. Removing tacks in direction of timber grain

It is wise before starting to strip off the covering to test the timber frame for any damaged or slack joints. With one knee firmly on the seat of the item, grip various parts of the upholstered frame and see if there is any noticeable movement, other than the movement of the upholstery, at the junctions of arms, backs, wings, etc.

With prior knowledge of a faulty joint, you can make additional clearance around the joint to undertake repairs. Frequently, just one or two joints will need attention. This situation is easily remedied by screwing steel reinforcing plates across the joint. Various types of plates are available (*figure* 7). These are quite thin if fixed to the outside line of the timber frame; if you cover them with one or two layers of wadding under the covering fabric and they are

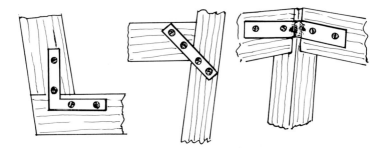

7. Use of steel reinforcing plates to strengthen frame joints

indiscernible. If possible, ease any slack joints open, remove old glue and apply fresh adhesive; then screw a reinforcing plate into position. A good suitable modern adhesive to use is P.V.A. adhesive. Although this is relatively quick drying, work should be halted for at least 12 hours to allow the adhesive to set thoroughly.

Should an upholstery frame be severely unstable because most of its joints are slack, a complete strip down of the upholstery will generally be required so that the joints can be attended to and cramped together using sash cramps or 'G' cramps (*figure* 8). A frame often becomes unstable when an upholstered piece gets wet and the adhesive breaks down.

Modern upholstery frames are constructed using the dowelled joint with one, two or three short pieces of dowel in each joint, dependent upon the section size of the timber; thicker timber, i.e. around the base of easy chairs and settees, has three dowels and slimmer rails have one dowel (*figure* 9).

When refurbishing and repairing older style or antique upholstery, you will often find mortice and tenon joints; if a tenon joint is damaged it is often broken at the neck. Unfortunately, this calls for a major operation of knocking the frame apart and replacing the complete rail with sound tenons, consequently disturbing the original upholstery.

8. Use of sash cramp to close front joints of chair

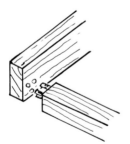 

9. Dowelled joints

Take care not to strip too much upholstery unnecessarily when refurbishing. Some of the basic work may be in sound condition, particularly if good quality materials were used in the first instance and the work was carried out well originally.

If a coil-sprung seat, the springs may need replacing and consequently the webbing. This will call for a complete strip out of the seat, but the arms and back of the item may well be sound and may be left undisturbed with just some fresh cotton wadding put over them, followed by the top covering.

Bent or buckled springs should never be straightened and re-used. In most cases the wire will have weakened and, within a short time, if re-used will revert back to its earlier crippled or bent shape. In fact, it is wise to discard all remaining coil springs if some have been distorted because the movement of the others will have been affected to a degree and there is a high risk that they, too, would also soon buckle.

I *Fireside and occasional chairs*

Contemporary fireside chairs and occasional chairs are mostly mass produced; they are made of polyurethane (plastic) or latex (rubber) foam and have some form of modern rubber or wire suspension to support the seat cushion. Unfortunately, foams and forms of rubber suspensions deteriorate and need renewing sooner than traditional materials that were used for upholstering a few decades ago.

Refurbishment and renewing foam cushions and fillings, together with the seat suspension, is relatively easy; providing the chair frame is in sound condition, a chair can soon be made to look as new with very little outlay. There is obviously an abundance of fireside and occasional chair styles that require various combinations of foam upholstery and differing kinds of seat support systems. By explaining some methods of renewing relevant parts within the following pages, I hope the reader will combine or adapt suggestions to suit his or her personal project.

REPLACING TENSION SPRINGS

Figure 10 shows tensions springs fitted to a fireside chair seat, hooked onto side plates screwed to each side member of the seat. Each spring (usually nine in total) is an elongated expanding spring and is hooked onto the side plates under tension, normally at 2.5 cm per 30.0 cm (1 in to 1 ft). The

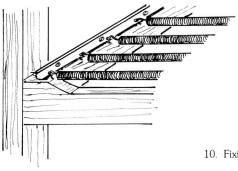

10. Fixing of tension springs

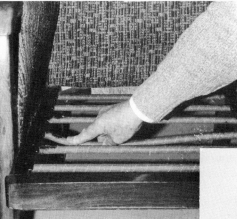

11. Unserviceable tension springs (slot fixing)

12. Rubber webbing replacing unserviceable tension springs

springs are available in a number of lengths to suit different widths of chair. Although these springs are still available from a number of upholstery suppliers, their use in current upholstery production has declined in favour of resilient rubber webbing. Tension springs are produced with a plastic sleeve covering their length or a woven cotton sleeve, which is more durable as plastic sleeving tends to split. The springs are also produced uncovered for use when you are putting a covering over the surface of the combined springs.

A disadvantage in using this type of springing, as you may have found, is that the springs will easily overstretch and become oversized and unserviceable if badly treated (*figure* 11). This often happens when children stand on them with a foot upon only one strand of spring. A further disadvantage is that, owing to the narrow width of the springs, only a proportion of the seat cushion is supported, causing a good deal of the cushion under-surface to be forced between the wide gaps between springs.

Should repairs be necessary to a tension-sprung seat, it is worth considering replacing all the springs with strands of resilient rubber webbing; this gives a much greater width of support for the cushion and is less likely to overstretch (*figure* 12). If replacement springs are available and are to be used it is simple to unhook the original springs and replace them with the new ones. It is important to have the correct length to give a satisfactory springiness to the seat.

Figure 13 shows the method of covering the front 'lip' section of the seat when it is intended to allow the seat cushion to rest upon tension springs or rubber webbing without any padding or covering insulation. Note that covering for the padded front is first tacked reverse-side up on the top surface of the front member, taken under the first spring or strand of rubber webbing, and then brought forward over foam and tacked on under the surface of the front seat rail. Fold it under whilst tacking to give a neat finish.

Covering for side members of seat should be machine hemmed before fixing in position; the hemmed edge is laid over to cover the ends of springs or tacked ends of webbing. Also fold these under if tacked on the underside

13. Method of upholstering front of chair

of frame. Normally joins between front section and sides
would be butted together with a mitre join and finally
slipstitched.

The example being worked upon and shown in the
illustrations has small covered arms; this may require a
different approach to the above open arm type of fireside
chair method. In this case the side borders are tacked on the
side face of the seat side member in the same position as the
base of the inside arm will be tacked. It is advisable to fix the
side borders on before the front as they can be tacked on
the front rail with the front crossing over above and running
down the side finishing with tacking off underneath.

REPLACING SPRINGS WITH RUBBER WEBBING
(*figures* 10, 14 and 15)

There are two widths of Pirelli rubber webbing readily available to the amateur upholsterer. Although various colours

are sometimes available from D.I.Y. stores, the neutral, putty coloured web is normally used for general work. Two widths are available: 51 mm (2 in) and 38 mm ($1\frac{1}{2}$ in). The wider width is suitable for webbing seats of fireside, easy chairs and settee seats covering relatively large spans; the narrower width is more suitable for backs of chairs and settees and for smaller furniture with loose seats, etc.

To replace the original tension springs with rubber webbing, remove the front border and side covering strips, lifting out tacks holding material on the underside of the frame. Unhook the lengths of springing from each side plate. There will be four or five screws holding the plates; remove the screws and discard the metal plates. With a wood rasp or coarse sandpaper remove the sharp corner on the top inside edge of the side member to prevent chaffing the web.

APPLYING RUBBER WEBBING

Tension rubber webbing when fixing it into position; this may be done by hand. Fix the webbing in position using a hammer and four or five 12 mm ($\frac{1}{2}$ in) tacks (*figure* 14); alternatively, use 8 mm ($\frac{3}{8}$ in) wire staples fired from a suitable strong staple firing tool with five or six staples fired into the webbing and timber in a slightly diagonal direction (not a straight line). See the other methods of attaching rubber webbing in figures 15 and 16.

Whereas linen or jute woven webbing should be folded and double-tacked at the fixing point to prevent fraying, rubber webbing, in view of its construction, will not fray at the ends. Consequently it needs only one line of tacks for securing the ends. Normally four or five tacks are sufficient for fixing 51 mm (2 in) webbing to sound timber. Ensure that the tack heads are hammered 'home' completely flat. If the head is tilted, it may cut into the rubber surface and weaken the fixing (*figure* 17). Different tensions may be given to rubber webbing, depending upon the firmness of the seat or the deflection or depth of 'sink' required. Each strand in a seat or back must be given the

14. Tensioning and tacking rubber webbing

15. Inserting rubber webbing with steel plate into side slot of chair seat

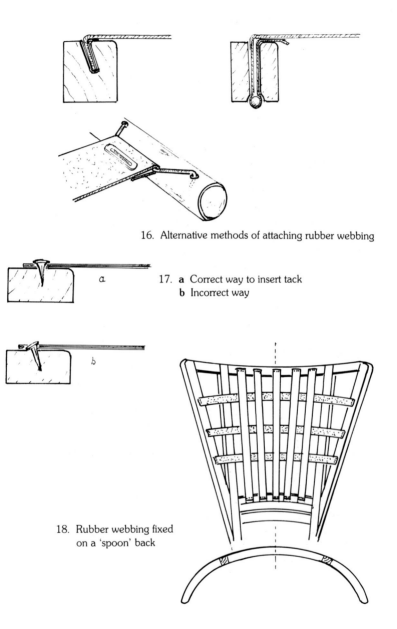

16. Alternative methods of attaching rubber webbing

17. **a** Correct way to insert tack
    b Incorrect way

18. Rubber webbing fixed
    on a 'spoon' back

RE-UPHOLSTERING A FIRESIDE CHAIR (*figure* 21)

The chair is badly in need of re-upholstery, the covering is badly soiled, the cushion has collapsed on the front edge, back foam has shredded, and the tension springs are unserviceable. Rubber webbing must be tacked on top surface of side seat members, and covered with a hemmed border. The front member must then be padded and covered (*figure* 13).

MATERIALS

     Rubber webbing (seat)—2.30 m (7 ft 6 in) × 5 cm (2 in)

     Rubber webbing (back, if necessary)—3.60 m (12 ft 0 in) × 3.6 cm ($1\frac{1}{2}$ in) or 2.75 m (9 ft 0 in) × 5 cm (2 in)

     Hessian—0.9 m (1 yd)

     Lining strip—1.50 m (5 ft 0 in) × 10 cm (4 in)

     Foam (back)—51 cm × 76 cm (1 ft 8 in × 1 ft 6 in)

     Foam cushion—46 cm × 46 cm (1 ft 6 in × 1 ft 6 in × 7.5 cm or 10 cm (3 in or 4 in)

     Foam arms (if necessary)—46 cm × 46 cm (1 ft 6 in × 1 ft 6 in) × 2 pieces

     Foam seat front—50 cm × 15 cm (1 ft 8 in × 6 in)

     Covering fabric—2.53 m ($2\frac{3}{4}$ yd) × 1.27 m (50 in) width

     Covered upholstery buttons for back if desired—3

     Tacks—13 mm ($\frac{1}{2}$ in) and 10 mm ($\frac{3}{8}$ in), or staples

     Adhesive

TOOLS

     Hammer or stapling tool

     Scissors

     Ripping chisel and mallet or substitutes

     Pliers or pincers

     Spatular for adhesive

     Bench vice if using steel plates for webbing

21. Fireside chair in need of refurbishing

The covering was found to be held by staples. These were easily removed using the narrow blade of a screwdriver and the foam and hessian were removed from the back. Black cotton felt padding on arms is re-usable so this was taken off and retained. Sinuous springs on the back were in good serviceable condition so were left undisturbed.

Tension springs were removed from seat and end hooks opened with the aid of a strong screwdriver. These were replaced with five strands of 5 cm (2 in) rubber webbing at $7\frac{1}{2}\%$ tension, tacked on the top surface of side seat members using 4–13 mm ($\frac{1}{2}$ in) fine tacks. The amount of tension was marked on each strand equally (*figure* 14).

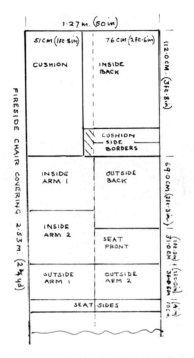

22. Cover cutting plan for fireside chair in figure 21

New hessian was tacked over the sinuous back springs using 13 mm ($\frac{1}{2}$ in) tacks, and edges of hessian were folded and double tacked for strength.

Back foam, of a thickness of 3.6 cm ($1\frac{1}{2}$ in), was cut to size using a broad blade knife; strips of lining 10 cm (4 in) wide were stuck along the long side edges above arm position and across top edge of back. After allowing drying time, the foam was positioned and stapled to the side back members (*figure* 2) and across the back side of the top member – this secures the foam sufficiently without any fixing below arm level.

Covering was then applied to back, laid across surface of foam, temporary tacked in first instance to outside top back member, smoothed down, tucked through and tacked to outside back stay rail (above seat rail). Sides were folded back to enable arm stiles to be cut (*see figure* 42) then tacked to outside back member above and below arms. When correctly positioned these were tacked off permanently.

Side borders to cover ends of webs were hemmed and tacked to front member, then strained to back of seat, the unhemmed side being tacked along side of seat member. Covering for front of seat was tacked to top of front rail and passed under first web (*figure* 13), brought forward over a thickness of foam to soften front edge, and then tacked folded under along base of front rail.

The original padding was used on the arms with two layers of skin wadding over it. Covering was fixed to underside of top arm, eased down, and tacked on the side of the seat member and the front cut-out shape behind the showwood arm stay, the rear of arm being tacked along side of back.

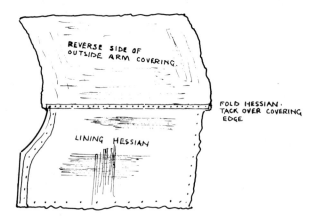

23. 'Back' tacking outside arm covering using lining hessian

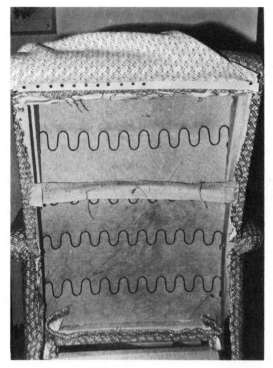

24. 'Back' tacking outside back covering using strip of card

Outside arms were back tacked (*figure* 23) using the top edge of lining hessian. (It is wise to use a reinforcing lining hessian on outside arm and outside back coverings.) The bottom line of the outside arm was folded under and tacked along the underside of the base rail. Outside back covering was back tacked using a strip of card to attain the line along top of back (*figure* 24). The covering was then folded down and tacked folded under on the underside of the base rail, sides of outside back being pinned into position and slipstitched or, alternatively, gimp pinned at intervals.

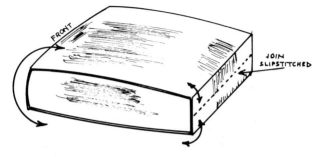

25. Fireside chair seat cushion with side panels

Cushion foam used was 10 cm (4 in) deep polyether foam. The covering was cut to the width of the seat between arms plus seaming allowance each side of 1 cm ($\frac{3}{8}$ in) and in one length from centre back border across top, down front

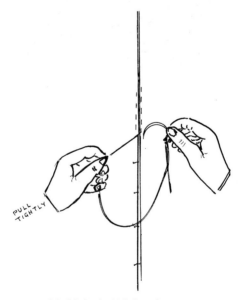

26. Method of 'slip' stitching covering

border, across base and back to centre back border again. This included an allowance for seaming join at the centre of the back cushion from side to side (*figure* 25). Two rectangular side borders were cut to fit side panels of foam cushion plus seaming allowance and machined to give a plain seam to each side. This, of course, could have been piped or ruched if desired. An opening to insert foam interior was left at the rear, across the complete width of the cushion; this was subsequently slipstitched after filling (*figure* 26). Figure 27 shows the completed fireside chair.

27. Refurbished fireside chair

RE-UPHOLSTERY OF AN OCCASIONAL CHAIR
(*figure* 28)

MATERIALS

Woven webbing, linen or jute—6.10 m (6.2–3 yd) seat and back

Seat springs (double cone)—9–15 cm (6 in) × 10 swg

Hessian—0.70 m ($\frac{3}{4}$ yd)

Linen scrim—0.75 m ($\frac{5}{6}$ yd)

Fibre/hair first stuffing seat—1.20 kg ($2\frac{1}{2}$ lb)

Hair second stuffing seat—0.35 kg ($\frac{3}{4}$ lb)

Back, if necessary, terylene fibre-fill—1.80 m (2 yd)

Sheet wadding—2 m (2 yd)

Bottoming—0.61 m (2–3 yd) hessian or linen

Tacks—16 mm ($\frac{5}{8}$ in), 13 mm ($\frac{1}{2}$ in), 10 mm ($\frac{3}{8}$ in)

Gimp pins—13 mm ($\frac{1}{2}$ in)

Adhesive

Cord for lashing springs—6 m (6 yd) flax, hemp or nylon

Covering fabric—1.50 m (1.2–3 yd) diagram 29

Thread for slipstitching

TOOLS

Hammer

Scissors

Ripping chisel and mallet or substitute

Webbing stretcher or substitute

Spring needle or large circular needle

Stitching needle 20–5 cm (8–10 in) length

Upholsterer's regulator

Spatular for adhesive

Small circular needle

Stripping chair

Figure 6 shows an occasional chair upturned with its seat resting upon a kitchen stool setting it at a convenient height for you to remove hessian bottoming. Hammer out the tacks working along length of side rail i.e. in the direction of grain

28. Refurbished occasional chair

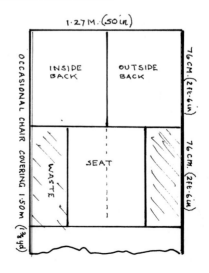

29. Cover cutting plan
for occasional
chair in figure 28

of timber – to avoid damage to underside of side member. Here, an old screwdriver is being used with the mallet.

With bottoming removed, you can examine the condition of webbing and springs. Additional webbing had been tensioned over the original webbing at some time during the life of the chair owing to its failure. Both sets of web needed replacing. Springs appeared to be misplaced and crippled with hessian split. It was necessary, therefore, to strip out completely the seat.

Repair of frame

Test the frame joints after removal of seat upholstery; in this case all were sound, except the two front joints at each end of the front rail, which were slightly open and loose. These two joints were carefully tapped open a little further, old adhesive was scraped out of joint and new P.V.A. adhesive inserted using a small paint brush; the joints were then cramped together using a sash cramp (*figure* 8). Use a small piece of cardboard or thin ply under the jaws of the cramp to prevent damage to the polished finish.

Figure 30 shows an alternative method of holding joints together whilst the adhesive sets; this is the Stanley frame clamp available at most D.I.Y. stores. It is necessary to ensure that the joints are well together when using this. Although it is efficient in pulling smaller frames together, it needs help when used on larger work, but it will keep the joints together whilst the adhesive dries.

Note that in figure 31 that wood corner braces have been fitted behind the front legs. These were cut, glued and screwed into position to strengthen the frame after cramping.

Webbing

With the chair upturned once again, 5×4 strands of linen webbing were tacked to the base of the chair using 16 mm ($\frac{5}{8}$ in) tacks. Figure 31 shows all strands interwoven with ends folded, the first end (front) and one side (right) with five tacks in a staggered formation on the double web fold, other ends of strands having three tacks under fold before

30. Alternative method of pulling frame joints together using cord cramp

31. Underside of occasional chair showing interlacing of linen webbing and sewing in of springs

folding, with two on the folded web. Webs are evenly spaced so that the base of all the springs is well supported.

Using the webbing stretching tool to tension webbing on the base of the chair is shown in figures 32 and 33. These show clearly how the tool is threaded with web to be able to attain the tightness necessary. The rebated bottom edge of the tool is held against the bottom edge of the base rail and the narrow handle section levered down to the appropriate tension required.

An alternative to using the standard webbing stretcher, but a little more difficult, is shown in figure 5 using a length of wood equal in width to the webbing. The webbing is folded over the length of wood forming a loop at the base of the wood; this loop is trapped between the frame and end of wood. Gripping the wood and webbing tightly, it is levered down so that the tensioned strand is lying across the back frame member in a position for tacking, as with the normal web stretcher.

32. Threading linen webbing into webbing stretcher

33. Webbing threaded into webbing stretcher ready for tensioning

Springing

Figure 31 also shows twine holding springs to webbing from the underside, with three knotted ties to each spring in triangular formation. Sew springs to the webbing using a spring or circular needle, working from the underside with chair standing correct way up on its feet (*see* p. 57).

Then lash seat springs in both directions (*figure* 34). If the normal flax or hemp upholstery laid cord is not available, use nylon cord at a thickness of 3 mm ($\frac{1}{8}$ in). Use 16 mm ($\frac{5}{8}$ in) tacks to hold lashing cords, temporary tacking them into position before starting the lashing process.

Fireside and occasional chairs

34. Lashed springs in occasional chair seat

Working from back member to front, measure and cut 3 strands of cord of suitable length to travel from back to front over the springs, plus an additional amount at each end for a return from the tacking position to knot to the top coil, plus an estimated amount that the clovehitch knotting (*figure* 35) will take (it is better to be a little generous). Start the lashing by tacking cords on the top surface of back seat member, not forgetting to leave a long end sufficient to knot to top coil.

Working from a standing position at the front of the chair, stretch over to the centre cord, tie it with a clovehitch knot to the second coil from the top, and then across the spring trying it to the opposite side of top coil. Lash the cord

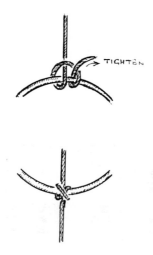

35. Forming the clovehitch knot

across the centre spring (with two knots), then tie it to top coil of front spring, then down to second coil, and tie and proceed to tack it on the front rail. There should be sufficient cord left to knot up to the top coil. Leave the return cords and tie them all to their respective positions after the main cross-lashings have been completed.

    Three points are important with spring lashing: (a) cords must be tensioned tightly; (b) the springs on the outside rows should be lashed with a slight tilt towards the tacking position – this is to counteract the strain towards the centre when weight is applied; and, (c) there should be no lateral movement when lashing is completed. After completing the forward lashing, work the strands side to side using the same principle.

    Lay hessian, minimum quality 366 g/m^2 (12 oz), over the lashed springs, with one line of tacks on top surface of each seat member; then trim it and fold it with a second line of tacks using 13 mm ($\frac{1}{2}$ in) tacks. Tension the hessian to maintain the height of springs but only lightly so as to remove only the looseness. Sew spring top coils to the hessian in the same way as sewing them to the webbing (*figure* 31).

Stuffing

At this stage there are two alternative methods of upholstery. (1) Forming a 'tack roll' on the front and two side members of the seat to get a soft edge, the height of upholstered edge being governed by the thickness of roll made (*figure* 36). This method is frequently used to simulate the stitched edges found in traditional upholstery made in earlier times, or, indeed, currently where craftsmanship is the main consideration or antique upholstery is being refurbished, since a tack-roll edge is a quicker method of getting a reasonably acceptable finish.

It will be seen in figure 36 that a tack-roll has been completed along the front member. This is approximately thumb sized, a suitable height in relation to the height of springs already sewn in the seat. The roll is being worked on the right hand member; towards the front you can see that the 13 cm (5 in) strip of hessian is tacked along the bevelled or rasped edge, the hessian being folded over at tacking line.

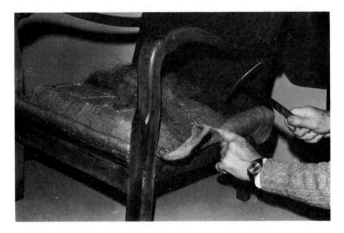

36. Making the 'tack' roll

Sufficient filling is laid along the edge to give the size of roll required, the hessian is then rolled over the filling, tucked in firmly, folded under and tacks hammered in along the folded edge (*figure* 36). Tacks 13 mm ($\frac{1}{2}$ in) should be used, spaced fairly closely at approximately 13 mm ($\frac{1}{2}$ in) to give an even smooth finish to the roll.

The seat is then filled with fibre, hair or other filling using bridle ties (*figure* 36). Ensure that the area immediately behind the roll is amply filled to avoid a channel, with sufficient filling over the springing to insulate them completely and avoid any likelihood of springs being felt through the filling. Scrim or hessian is pulled over the filling, firstly temporary tacked, and then tacked home. In the case of a rebate along the front edge, the scrim or hessian would be tacked carefully along this rebate. Stuffing ties should then be run through the scrim or hessian, filling and spring hessian, as in figures 37 and 38. The seat is now ready for its second stuffing.

(2) The alternative to this is traditional stuffing and stitching. Figures 37 and 38 show the seat being stitched with the long upholsterer's stitching needle; a 'fine' or bayonet point needle may be used. The bayonet point has a rather thicker end with a triangular three-faced pointed end rather than a long fine smooth point, which is more suitable for buttoning work.

To proceed with this method after you have put the hessian over the springs ensure that there is a bevel or chamfer on the top edge of seat members, sufficiently wide to take the head of a tack. This can be made with a wood rasp. Use Algerian black fibre, coir fibre or horsehair as filling in the stitched version of the seat. Pack filling firmly under bridle ties (loops sewn into the hessian as in *figures* 36 and 38), with a slight doming to the centre. Temporary tack scrim, or loosely woven hessian as a second choice, on front and two sides. Tuck the back of the scrim through under back stay rail, ensuring the weave is perfectly straight in both directions.

Sew twine stuffing ties using the 20/25 cm (8/10 in) needle through the surface of scrim, filling and spring hessian. When the needle passes through the spring hessian

37. Forming the 'blind' stitch

38. Forming the 'top' stitch, bridle ties are visible

return it after moving it approximately 5 mm ($\frac{1}{4}$ in) back through the scrim surface. The point of the needle will, of course, have to be passed through webbing before the end with twine threaded crosses the filling and hessian. The stuffing ties should form a running line with a continuous length of twine with knots only at the start and finish. Before knotting off, tension the twine tightly so that it sinks into the filling. Figures 37 and 38 show these ties.

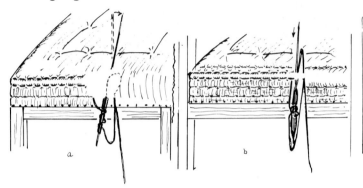

39. Twisting twine around the needle **a** blind stitch **b** top stitch

Now tack the scrim folded *under* using 6 mm ($\frac{3}{8}$ in) tacks on the bevelled edge. Filling should be firm enough with sufficient scrim allowed to give the height of edge required. Tacking should follow faithfully along one strand of weave. Two rows of stitching are shown in figure 38. One is the blind stitch and the other the roll or top stitch. Stitching is normally worked from left to right; figures 39 a and b show how these stitches are formed. An upholsterer's regulator can be seen protruding from the seat in figure 38. This is kept handy and used when stuffing needs regulating – that is, moving slightly within the scrim to attain a more even line.

Sew bridle ties in the surface of the stuffed seat (*figure* 38), which you have infilled with hair or other filling suitable as a second stuffing (*figure* 40) tapering it down to

40. Tucking filling under bridle ties

the stitched edges with slight doming to centre. An under-
cover is advisable stretched over and firstly temporary
tacked and then tacked home using 10 mm ($\frac{3}{8}$ in) tacks. If
you use horsehair as second stuffing, lay two layers minimum of sheet wadding over the undercover before you
apply the main covering.

Figure 41 shows how seat covering is folded back for
cutting of stiles, with chalk lines to show direction of cuts.
Surplus fabric each side of the cut is tucked down between
filling and frame.

Back

Webbing and hessian in the back needed replacing. Originally 1 × 1 strands were used and these were replaced with
two vertical and one horizontal webs with new hessian over

41. Cutting seat covering around arm and back 'stiles'

webbing. The horizontal web was tensioned by hand, although only lightly to conform to the slight hollow curve of the back. The original back filling was re-usable and in a complete layer – this was re-placed over the new base.

Covering was temporary tacked top and bottom with sides folded as figure 42 for cutting the covering around arm and leg stiles. The cutting lines are shown on the folded cover. The cut edges are folded under tightly around the arm and tacked on outside back.

Reinforcing hessian was tacked over outside back area using 10 mm ($\frac{3}{8}$ in) tacks. Covering at top of outside back was back tacked using a strip of card (*figure* 24). A layer of wadding was laid over hessian and the covering smoothed down over it and tacked on underside of base; the sides were firstly pinned into position and then slipstitched.

42. Cutting back covering around arm 'stiles'

Hessian bottom was tacked on the underside and the edges were folded under approximately 1 cm ($\frac{3}{8}$ in) from edges of frame using 10 mm ($\frac{3}{8}$ in) tacks.

II *Tub and 'spoon' back chairs*

The upholstering of tub or spoon back chairs (curved back chairs) presents rather more problems than normal straight or flat surfaced items. With curved backs of chairs, sometimes in two directions, you often have to tailor the covering to get an unwrinkled and smooth finish.

43. Upholstered tub chair

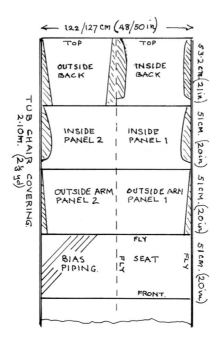

44. Cover cutting plan for tub chair, diagram 43, showing approximate shape of panels after tailoring

It is not possible to cover completely the back of the chair (*figure* 43) with one complete width or length of covering fabric. Owing to the curve and angle of the back frame, using one piece of fabric results in severe wrinkling or 'fullness' vertically around the shaped curve. To avoid this, tailor the back covering in three sections, cutting away the surplus fabric which would cause the wrinkling (*figure* 44) and sew the sections together.

Alternatively, on deeper upholstery of curved backs (*figure* 45) sewing in covered buttons forming diamond shapes will retain the curvature of the back. This, in fact, was the original purpose of applying buttoning to upholstery, rather than today's decorative purpose.

There are some important points to be considered when attempting the tub-shaped style of upholstery (*figure* 43).

When stripping down covering or basic upholstery for refurbishing the tub chair, particularly the back, take extreme care not to damage the frame members. Figure 46 shows a typical tub chair frame used for traditional upholstering. Note that the only straight frame members are the two front legs and front rail of the seat. Remaining members of the frame are curved or partially curved with very short

45. Buttoned 'spoon' back chair

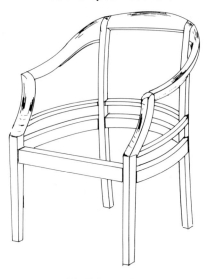

46. Tub chair frame

grain at certain sections, particularly the thin stay rails just above the main seat members. These thin stay rails are liable to shatter across the short grain if dealt with too severely – that is, if they are hammered too heavily if too large a tack is put in the section of the rail. Only 10 mm ($\frac{3}{8}$ in) tacks should be used on the curved stay rails for webbing, hessian (canvas), calico undercovering and top covering. In fact, 10 mm ($\frac{3}{8}$ in) tacks will suffice for all the work other than on the thicker seat rails, which will have webbing and other seat materials tacked upon them.

The thin curvature of the back upholstery (*figure* 43) must be maintained to preserve the character of the chair. To achieve this effect apply minimum depth of filling to the back; tension the undercovering and top covering mainly vertically or from base of the back to top, and smooth the covering just lightly either horizontally or from side to side to keep it flat on the base filling and stop it from being lifted away from it.

Cut both side panels of the back and each side of the centre panel as identical shapes. To achieve this, draw a centre line down the centre of the back.

Firstly, to shape the calico under-covering draw the centre line in biro onto the hessian lining the centre section of the frame. Tack a length of twine to the centre of the inner face of one of the back legs just below stay rail level, draw the twine up tightly to centre of back leg at top of the back and tack twine on the outside of the back. This twine line will give a suitable joining line for centre and side panels for the under-covering.

With a suitable sized piece of calico or similar under-cover material for the centre panel, make a fold vertically down the centre of the fabric, keeping the fold on one line of thread (to ensure equal shaping of threads at each side when cut). Temporary tack the folded material with the fold along the centre biro line on the hessian, temporary tacking with one tack only at top and bottom. Smooth the folded fabric across to the twine line, again inserting a temporary tack at top and bottom to hold the material steady whilst being cut. An extra allowance of 1 cm ($\frac{3}{8}$ in) must be made at the join line on both the centre and side panels for machine joining. After cutting the centre panel, cut the side panel (double thickness to achieve a pair in one operation). Firstly, temporary tack it into position and then cut to the twine line, not forgetting the machining allowance. The cut lines on each panel should gently curve without any sudden deviations, other than at the base (*figure* 44) where allowance is made to curve under the stay rail.

Whilst centre and side panels are still in position on the back, snip three notches or small vees along the cut edges, one spaced centrally and one approximately 10 cm (4 in) from each end, so that when removed for machining, the notches may be aligned and the shapes correctly positioned. The centre panel should have an equally curved shape on both side edges when unfolded. The calico under-covering should have a plain seam only, but seams of the top covering should be piped using thin 3 mm ($\frac{1}{8}$ in) piping cord. A short length of piping should be left, extending beyond the top and bottom edges of the covering, so that you can grip it firmly to tension the piping vertically.

Tailor the top covering in the same way after the back infilling has been applied and tack the under-covering into position. The outside back and side sections must also be tailored.

It is particularly important that the covering for piping the back is cut on the bias (*figure* 44). This will allow an equal movement of the piping with the back and side panels when being tensioned. Should the piping fabric be cut following straight threads of the weave, it will not stretch with the shaped cuts of the back; it will invariably lock fullness and cause puckering along the sewn line of centre and side panels which cannot be removed by tensioning the piping or covering.

RE-UPHOLSTERY LAND RE-COVERING A TUB CHAIR (*figure* 43)

TOOLS

        Hammer
        Scissors
        Ripping tool
        Hammer/mallet
        Spring or large circular needle
        Small circular needle
        Web tensioning tool
        20/25 cm (8/10 in) long needle (bayonet)

In most instances a tub chair back, such as that illustrated, is usually in sound condition; if being re-covered it will need only the covering removing without any further major work done on the back. Backs of leather-covered tub chairs tend to develop wrinkling in the centre panel due to stretching of the leather over years of use. This wrinkling can often be removed by re-tensioning the piping or welting between centre and side panels and easing out the loose leather over the top rail after releasing the top outside back.

The state of tub chair seats is usually the major cause of re-upholstering. Where coil springs have been used, the springs may have buckled or become displaced; woven webbing may have deteriorated and thus broken away from the tacks holding the strands in position.

MATERIALS NEEDED TO COMPLETELY RE-UPHOLSTER

Webbing—linen or jute 7.50 m (8 yd)

Coil springs—9–13   cm (5 in) × 10 swg (standard wire gauge)

Hessian (canvas)—1 m × 1.83 m width (1 yd × 6 ft 0 in width)

Scrim—0.60 m × 0.60 m (2 ft 0 in × 2 ft 0 in)

Fibre filling (seat)—1 kg ($2\frac{1}{4}$ lb)

Horsehair (seat and back)—0.90 kg (2 lb)

Calico or lining under-cover—60 cm × 1.83 m width ($\frac{2}{3}$yd)

Skin wadding—3.75 m × 0.46 m width (4 yd × 1 ft 6 in width)

Bottoming—0.50 m × 0.50 m (1 ft 8 in × 1 ft 8 in)

Covering—2.10 m × 1.22–1.27 m width ($2\frac{1}{3}$ yd × 48–50 in width)

Gimp or braid—1.85 m (2 yd)

plus tacks 10 mm ($\frac{3}{8}$ in fine) and 12 mm ($\frac{1}{2}$ in fine)

Twine and adhesive

Lashing cord

MATERIALS TO RE-UPHOLSTER SEAT ONLY

Webbing (linen or jute)—4 m ($4\frac{1}{3}$ yd)

Coil springs—9–13 cm (5 in) × 10 swg

Hessian—0.50 m × 0.50 m (1 ft 8 in × 1 ft 8 in)

Scrim—0.60 m × 0.60 m (2 ft 0 in × 2 ft 0 in)

Fibre filling—1 kg ($2\frac{1}{4}$ lb)

Horsehair—0.50 kg ($1\frac{1}{4}$ lb)

Calico or lining under-cover—0.56 m × 0.56 m (1 ft 10 in × 1 ft 10 in)

Skin wadding—1 m × 0.46 m (1 yd × 1 ft 6 in)

Bottoming—0.50 m × 0.50 m (1 ft 8 in × 1 ft 8 in)

Gimp or braid 1.85 m (2 yd)

Tacks—12 mm ($\frac{1}{2}$ in) fine

Lashing cord

Twine and adhesive

Plan and cut covering fabric as shown in figure 44. Each of the inside and outside backs and side panels should be cut from the half width in the first instance and tailored into shape afterwards. Do this either as described on pp. 49–50 or, if possible, carefully remove the back covering with the three sections intact – the stitching may be cut through to separate the three sections. These sections may then be used as templates for cutting the new covering. The same applies to the outside covering which should also be in three sections.

Stripping down a tub chair

Assuming you have not decided to strip off completely all materials owing to deterioration, leave any materials you find sound in position.

Upturn the tub chair with the seat resting on a stool or box of suitable height – this will help you remove tacks which are holding the bottoming fabric. Work with the grain of the timber using a ripping chisel and mallet or old screwdriver and hammer. On removal of the bottom, hammer out the tacks which are holding the outside covering around the base and tacks holding front of the seat (if it is not tacked into a rebate on the face).

Turn the chair up on its legs and cut the slipstitching holding the outside covering around the outer edges of the chair back, and remove trimming. This may be either piping or ruching. In most cases there will be reinforcing hessian tacked on the outside of the frame. This should be completely removed – it is not worth leaving this partially hanging in place. Outside edges of the seat will now be accessible. Remove all tacks holding all the seat materials tacked on the upper face of the seat members and across the front seat rail. Cut away all twines, including twines holding springs in position. Take out springs and remove the webbing from underside of chair.

The back of chair can now be stripped; remove covering, wadding, under-covering, filling, lining hessian and webbing, leaving the bare frame. Clean away any odd splinters of wood which may be protruding and any partially extracted tacks.

Re-upholstering

It is more convenient to start work on the back of the tub chair first; this will allow easy access to the base or back stay rail where the covering needs to be taken through under the stay rail and tacked on the back face. This part becomes very difficult with the seat in position. Should you be re-covering only the chair, you must force down firmly the back and sides of the seat to get the back covering through under the stay rail.

Back webbing

Two vertical and one horizontal webs should be applied to the centre panel rails; the two vertical webs should be spaced evenly and tacked carefully on the face of the stay rail with a fold using 10 mm ($\frac{3}{8}$ in) tacks. Should there be difficulty hammering tacks on the inner face of this rail owing to bad housing of the joints (this sometimes occurs), take the webbing under the rail and tack it on the outside of the curve. Hammering on the outside will tend to force the joint back into its housing. These two webs should be only hand tensioned as tightly as possible and tacked on the inside face of the top back rail. It is better not to make a fold at this end to avoid an obvious bump under the sparse filling at the top of the back. Place the horizontal web *behind* both vertical webs. This may have a fold at both ends. This web should be only lightly handstrained so as not to draw the vertical webs forward.

Tack two lengths of web vertically on both inner side panels, tacking from the stay rail to the inner back rail; again only hand tension the web with no fold at the top fixing point.

Hessian lining

After webbing, line the three sections with hessian, working centre panel separately first, then the two side panels. Firstly, tack hessian on stay rails using 10 mm ($\frac{3}{8}$ in) tacks, then tension it to the top back rails by hand as tightly as possible. Ease out the looseness by working lightly side to side. Trim the hessian leaving sufficient to fold over and tack this excess back with a second row of tacks.

Tailoring under-cover

The calico or lining under-cover should be prepared at this stage, cut and tailored as described on pp. 49–50, and the three sections machined together with plain seam.

Sew bridle ties, using fine twine, into the hessian with loops approximately 15 cm (6 in) apart. These should run vertically around the radius of the back. As the filling will be rather thinly applied, the bridle ties will need very little slackness left in the loops – just sufficient to allow a small handful of filling to be anchored beneath the loop of twine.

Back stuffing

The old filling, usually of horsehair, should be 'teased' – that is, strands loosened and opened with the fingers. This should then be put in the back and tucked into the bridle tie loops; they will thus hold the filling in position whilst being worked. Fill the centre back in the first instance from bottom stay rail to top back, thinning it out as it nears the outer edge; then work it round to side panels, ensuring that each side has equal filling.

Horsehair should be applied quite thinly in depth, approximately 2.5 cm (1 in) only if a good quality horsehair is being used. A lesser quality would need a little more depth.

To assess the quality of horsehair, hold a small quantity in the fingers of both hands, slowly moving your hands apart to extend the sample. The curled strands of hair will extend for a considerable length, perhaps 24 cm (9 in) or so and be well curled. The strands of a poorer quality mixture of horse and hoghair, or hoghair solely, given the same treatment, will separate, fall apart and drop from your fingers. Good quality horsehair will consist of the long strands of mane and tail hair, which can be well curled. This accounts for its excellent resiliency.

Under-covering

When applying under-covering it is important to centre mark both the frame and fabric to ensure that seams are placed equally on each side of centre. Temporary tack top

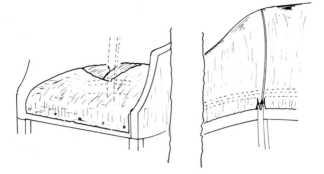

47. Cutting around back leg stiles of tub chair

centre of back – in the first instance fabric may be temporary tacked on the inside of the back stay rail whilst positioning. After cutting around the leg stiles (*figure* 47) take the bottom line of under-cover through under the stay rail and tack it on the back face using 10 mm ($\frac{3}{8}$ in) tacks. After tacking around base of back, tightly tension the under-covering vertically and tack home working from centre to each front corner. Then tack front edge of side panels – these need easing only lightly to remove wrinkling and they should not be tensioned to any degree.

Back covering
Now proceed to tailor the back covering in the same manner as preparing the under-cover with two twines pulled vertically from centre of back legs, centre at stay rail height and top of back. Allow fractionally less seaming allowance at the centres of the curves with covering for a distance of approximately 15 cm (6 in), reverting gradually to the normal 1 cm ($\frac{3}{8}$ in) towards both ends of the seam. This helps remove any likely fullness in the sewn back whilst it is fixed in position. Seams of the covering should be piped or ruched.

A minimum of two layers of skin wadding should be laid over the under-covering before applying the top covering. Wadding should be laid on with the minimum of creases. It is advisable to tear the wadding into three sections around the curve of the back, thinly overlapping the edge of wadding. Avoid disturbing the wadding when placing the covering in position. A good tension is required vertically on the piping or ruching, whichever is being used.

Upholstering the seat

Webbing for a coil-sprung seat should be on the underside of the frame. For a normal sized tub chair as illustrated, 4 × 3 strands minimum are required. Linen or jute webbing may be used. Linen webbing is the better of the two and is black and white with a herringbone pattern stripe; this, however, is more expensive than the brown plain woven jute type. The extra cost of linen web is, however, more than justified.

Webbing should be interlaced as in figure 31 and tacked using 12 mm ($\frac{1}{2}$ in) tacks as shown in figure 48. An upholsterer's webbing stretching tool is normally used to

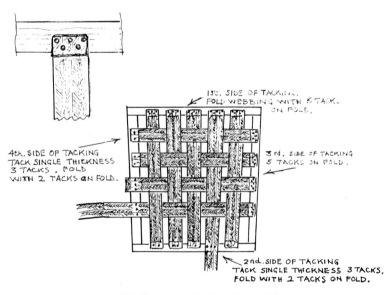

48. Sequence of tacking linen webbing

tension woven webbing, but a piece of wood may be used as a substitute (*figure* 5).

Care should be taken not to over-tension webbing as this could damage the weave of the webbing; also avoid ripping the webbing from its holding tacks or distorting the chair frame and damaging its joints. A suitable test of correct tensioning is; whilst gradually increasing pressure on the tensioning tool, to tap the webbing with the side of the hammer head. Whilst the webbing is still slack there will be a dull sound from the webbing. This will gradually change as the webbing is tightened to a drumming sound. Generally at this stage webbing is sufficiently tight and is ready to be tacked to the frame.

Seat springs

Normally 9–12.5 cm (5 in) × 10 swg springs are needed for the seat. These should be spaced evenly across the webbing, being sewn by the bottom coil onto the webbing from the underside using good quality flax twine. Three knotted ties should be made onto each bottom coil in triangular form, by passing the spring (or circular) needle through the webbing from the underside, drawing the twine through webbing adjacent to the coil wire, and then down through the web again on the opposite side of the wire coil. Hold the loop of twine as it hangs under the webbing, then as the needle returns through the base, pass the needle through the loop to form a knot. This should be pulled tight at each position. It does not matter if the length of twine exhausts before sewing in all the springs as a fresh length may be started at any position.

Top coils of springs should be lashed or tied across in both directions (*figure* 34); this is to avoid any lateral movement which could cause a spring to buckle during use. Upholsterer's flax or hemp laidcord is normally used for this purpose. Sisal cord is the correct thickness but not durable enough. Tacks of 16 mm ($\frac{5}{8}$ in) are preferable for tacking cord lashing to seat rails to get a good anchorage on the top surface of front, back and side seat members. Nylon cord is a good substitute for flax cord.

Working from back to front, on the initial tacking of the cord leave a free length sufficient to reach the top coil with enough to tie a knot; start the lashing going to the second coil from the top with a clovehitch knot (*figure* 35); then go to the top coil at opposite side of spring, knot, and proceed across. Knot each side of top coil centre spring, last spring at last knot, down to second coil from top, and then down to the tacking point. Do this with each spring in both directions. Lash end springs in each row with a fractional tilt to the outside line of the seat – this is to counteract the drag into the centre when the seat is sat upon.

With the seat springs secure, hessian (minimum quality 366 g/m^2 (12 oz)) should be laid over and tacked to the top surface of seat members using 12 mm ($\frac{1}{2}$ in) tacks. Tension the hessian across the springs' surface without reducing the height of springs. Tack single thickness and then fold back the excess. Then tack a further line of tacks for strength so that you have double tacked on each seat member.

Using a spring or large circular needle and fine twine, sew top coils of springs through the hessian in a similar form to that done on the underside of the webbing with three knotted ties in triangular formation (*figure* 31). Push the point of the needle into the hessian on one side of the spring wire, pass it under the wire and out again forming a loop around the spring. By turning a twist of twine around the needle as it lifts out and is withdrawn, form a knot – a little practice may be needed to do this quickly.

Now sew twine bridle ties (loops) into the hessian, two loops on each of the four sides running parallel with the sides but approximately 7.5 cm (3 in) in from edges, also running two loops down centre of seat back to front.

Seat filling

Leave the bridle ties sufficiently slack to tuck a small handful of filling under. A good guide is to lay a hand on the spring hessian and let the twine loop over the hand – this will usually give sufficient slackness.

Apply teased filling firstly around sides and back of

seat, then across front edge of seat, and finally fill in centre producing a slight doming effect. Filling should be deep enough to insulate surface of springing and stop the top coils being felt through it.

Upholsterer's scrim (or, if unobtainable, loosely woven hessian) should be laid loosely over filling and tucked through sides and back under the stay rail. The scrim will need cutting at both back leg stiles, diagram 47. Back and sides of the scrim will normally be held tightly by the restricted clearance around sides and back, but along the front rail it will need temporary tacking initially with five or six 12 mm ($\frac{1}{2}$ in) tacks. Weave of scrim should run perfectly parallel with front edge rail.

Now sew twine stuffing ties through the surface of the scrim using a 20–24.5 cm (8–10 in) long needle. These should be taken through the filling and spring hessian, catching approximately 0.5 cm ($\frac{1}{4}$ in) of hessian, and passed back through the scrim again appearing on the surface 0.5 cm from the entry point. Run twine through at a number of positions to serve as a running line; pull it tight without knotting it, except for the first tie and last after the twine has been pulled tight throughout its length (*figure* 37).

Now tack the front edge of the scrim home and fold it *under* whilst tacking it with 10 mm ($\frac{3}{8}$ in) tacks onto the bevelled top edge of front rail. A bevel or chamfer can be made using a wood rasp or surform tool. It should be just sufficiently wide to allow the head of a tack to be hammered home on the extreme edge.

Stitching and under-covering

Ensure that the filling is sufficiently firm and deep enough to attain the desired height after stitching. Three rows of stitching will normally be required (*figure* 39), using the 20–24.5 cm (8–10 in) long needle.

With the stitching completed, scrim should be tacked 'off' and *folded under* at sides and back of seat. Insert bridle ties into the scrim surface in the same manner as in the spring hessian but a little tighter to accommodate a shallower depth of filling. Place a second thinner layer of filling under the ties slightly domed, and cover this with calico or thin material suitable for under-covering. Again, make cuts in the material to by-pass leg stiles (*figure* 47). Temporary tack well the under-cover in the first instance to get the correct tensioning, after which tack home using 12 mm ($\frac{1}{2}$ in) tacks on sides and back and 10 mm ($\frac{3}{8}$ in) along front edge.

Seat covering

Lay a minimum of two layers of sheet wadding over the seat under-covering to prevent hair strands working through the seat covering. Covering the seat is a similar operation to that of under-covering, but it is most important to align fabric weave straight in both directions.

Outside covering

With the inside covering work completed satisfactorily, line outside panels with hessian as a reinforcement for the covering. The original hessian may be good enough to re-use. Using 10 mm ($\frac{3}{8}$ in) tacks, work centre panel first tacking along top of hessian approximately half way down back member. Tension to base (no tension should be given horizontally) and tack hessian just as it touches back legs on each side. Hessian of side panels should be tacked again along top, following back shape, and tensioned to bottom rail.

Tailor the outside covering in three sections as the inside covering, using twine drawn tightly and the centre leg at top and one side of leg at base as the cutting line. Do not forget to add sewing allowance of 1 cm ($\frac{3}{8}$ in). This machine line may be a plain seam, piped or ruched if desired to match the inner seams. The same trimming may be tacked around the outside line of the tub chair.

Place a thickness of sheet wadding over the hessian with a tack here and there to hold it in position. Pin the outside covering in position with stout dressmaking pins. Do not use temporary tacking for this as tacks may leave a mark in the covering. Now tack the outside covering around the base members and cover the raw edges and tacks with a bottoming fabric, preferably black linen.

The pinned fabric around the outside edge should be finished off by slipstitching (*figure 26*). Finally, apply gimp or braid trimming around the base of the chair, fixing it with an adhesive such as Copydex.

BUTTONED 'SPOON' BACK CHAIR

TOOLS

        Hammer
        Scissors
        Ripping tool
        Hammer or mallet
        Spring or large circular needle
        Small circular needle
        Web tensioning tool
        20/25 cm (8/10 in) long bayonet needle and the same size fine buttoning needle
        Tailor's chalk

Figure 45 shows a typical Victorian spoon back chair with deep diamond buttoning to the back with a coil sprung seat. Invariably, it is the seat that needs re-upholstering and the back is often in reasonable condition, with the diamond buttoning partially flattened and pleating of the covering disturbed.

Figure 49 shows a transection of the upholstery of seat and back with basic frame construction. This type of Victorian spoon back chair may sometimes have small upholstered arms or just show-wood arms with a small upholstered arm pad. It may also have a polished rebated edge around the base with tacks hidden by gimp.

An original, well-upholstered example will have the buttoned back upholstered with good quality horsehair filling which can be re-used or re-teased whilst still in position. The seat may also be completely stuffed with horsehair over the springs.

A poorer quality example may have a filling of cotton flocks or cotton shoddy in the back and seat with perhaps alva (dried seaweed frequently used in Victorian up-holstery), in the basic 'first' stuffing of the seat over the coil springs. Unfortunately, both of these fillings are not suitable for re-use and should be discarded and replaced. You can, however, leave the back filling in place and place a further layer of horsehair and wadding over; alternatively, you can put one or two layers of 'fibre-fill' under the new covering.

49. Cut-through section of buttoned 'spoon' back chair

Replacement materials needed to completely re-upholster
Listed below are the approximate quantities, list 1 being total materials and list 2 being replacment materials for a deteriorated seat with basic back upholstery in sound condition.

List 1: Webbing (linen or jute)—9 m ($9\frac{1}{2}$ yd)
         Springs—9–15 cm (6 in) × 10 swg double cone springs
         Hessian—1 m × 1.83 m width (1 yd × 6 ft 0 in width)
         First stuffing hair or fibre for seat—1.75 kg ($3\frac{1}{2}$ lb)
         Scrim—0.76 m × 0.91 m (2 ft 6 in × 3 ft 0 in)
         Horsehair for second stuffing seat plus hair for back—3.20 kg (7 lb)
         Calico or lining under-covering—0.76 m × 0.91 m (2 ft 6 in × 3 ft 0 in)
         Covering—1.80 m (2 yd) (*figure* 50)
         Bottoming—0.61 m × 0.61 m (2 ft 0 in × 2 ft 0 in)
         Skin wadding—1 roll
         Buttons—18
         Gimp—2 m ($2\frac{1}{3}$ yd)
         Adhesive
         Fine twine, cord (lashing)
         Tacks—16 mm ($\frac{5}{8}$ in), 12 mm ($\frac{1}{2}$ in), 10 mm ($\frac{3}{8}$ in)

List 2: Webbing—5 m ($5\frac{1}{2}$ yd)
         Springs—9 × 15 cm (6 in) × 10 swg double cone springs
         Hessian—0.60 m × 0.60 m (2 ft 0 in × 2 ft 0 in)
         Fibre or hair first stuffing—1.75 kg ($3\frac{1}{2}$ lb)
         Scrim—0.76 m × 0.91 m (2 ft 6 in × 3 ft 0 in)
         Hair second stuffing—0.90 kg (2 lb)
         Calico or lining under-cover—0.76 m × 0.91 m (2 ft 6 in × 3 ft 0 in)
         Skin wadding—2.75 m (3 yd)
         Tacks—16 mm ($\frac{5}{8}$ in), 12 mm ($\frac{1}{2}$ in), 10 mm ($\frac{3}{8}$ in)
         Twine, cord, adhesive

Stripping down Victorian spoon back buttoned chair
With the chair upturned, remove tacks from around edges of bottoming fabric and also tacks holding base of outside back and sides and front of seat. Turn the chair up on its feet and cut away slipstitching holding outside back in position. This will enable you to remove the outside, together with

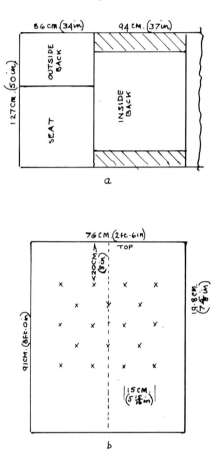

50. **a** Cover cutting plan for 'spoon' back chair **b** Marking of button positions on back covering

wadding that should be underneath. Also, the reinforcing hessian tacked over the frame should be completely removed, laying visible the twine ties and butterflies (*figure* 51) holding buttons in position. At this stage you can see if the back hessian is in sound enough condition to leave

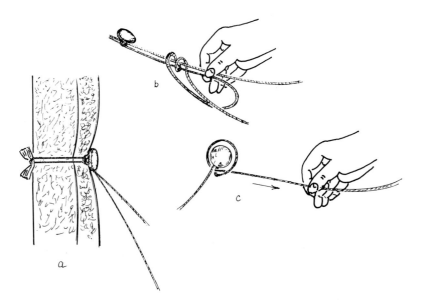

51. **a** Use of 'butterfly' in buttoning twine **b** Tying 'slip' knot **c** Tying off button twine

undisturbed of if it requires replacement. Do not be in too much of a hurry to remove it as it may not need replacing.

Leave the back now to concentrate on stripping all materials away from the seat, assuming this is in need of complete re-upholstery with new materials. Work systematically, removing one piece at a time, knocking tacks out *with* the grain of the timber and cutting twine ties out as they appear.

Should the seat be upholstered with good quality horsehair salvage the hair by removing all the pieces of twine and refuse and then tease and pull it apart with your fingers. This is a task best suited to the open air as the hair will contain an amount of dust; also wear a mask to prevent inhaling the dust. Filling other than horsehair should be discarded and fresh obtained.

Clean off any protruding splinters from the frame left whilst removing tacks, using a wood rasp or piece of coarse glasspaper; start webbing with the chair upturned with the seat frame resting on a trestle or box so that the webbing may easily be tacked on the underside of seat frame.

Webbing seat

Seat webbing should be the best available – if possible, good quality black and white linen, using five strands front to back with four across. Tack the webbing with 16 mm ($\frac{5}{8}$ in) tacks with five tacks at each web end (see web tacking sequence, *figure* 48). Firstly, apply centre web front to back, then the two extreme side webs, following with two in the wide spaces; this helps to space the webs equally. Working side to side, apply front web first, not forgetting to interlace webs alternately. Position the rear web in a suitable place in relation to spring positions, then place the remaining two webs between front and back webs the same distance apart. As mentioned in previous examples, webbing should *not* be over-tensioned; test it using the hammer as described.

Turning the chair back on to its feet and up to a convenient height, now sew springs onto the webs as described on p. 57. Should the seat be exceptionally wide, having large gaps between the nine springs, an additional row of three springs may be added, making four rows front to back. The springs should be securely lashed in both directions with hessian tacked over as described on pp. 58 and in figure 34.

Proceed with sewing spring top coils to the hessian and sewing in ample bridle ties with three overlapping loops across with four double loops front to back. Firmly place filling under the ties around edges and back with lighter domed filling in the centre. Initially, filling should overhang edges; ease it back with your fingers as the covering scrim is temporary tacked around front and sides. The back of the filling is tucked through under the stay rail.

Mark positions for stuffing ties (*figures* 37–38) onto the scrim, using point of a long needle, opening the weave of scrim to make a mark. The weave will remain open whilst you work for a short time. Mark four ties across, three front to back with three centre ties; these should be in a running line as mentioned in the last example.

Possibly the most difficult operation to master is tacking down scrim on a bow-shaped front edge. Normally on a straight seat edge scrim is tacked following the straight weave whereas on a shaped-front edge you must allow for the bowing but also keep the scrim at the correct height and the weave in alignment on the top surface of the scrim. The scrim should be tacked as on p. 4 and fixed with three rows of stitching – that is, blind stitch, roll stitch and top stitch. The remainder of the upholstery of seat is as pp. 59–60.

Upholstery of back

If the back is to be re-covered only, you can now remove the back covering and proceed with it. If you completely strip it for re-upholstering, re-web it with three strands vertical and four strands horizontal; place all the latter *behind* the vertical webs to preserve the concave shape of the back. Tension hessian tightly from the bottom stay rail to the top back, with just a light easing across to the back leg, and tack it. Sew a length of hessian or scrim approximately 23 cm (9 in) wide onto the base hessian of the back approximately 12 cm (5 in) from outside line of the back. This should be filled with fibre or hair with the hessian or scrim tacked on the outside of the frame; this will make a padded roll forming a well in the centre area of the back, which also helps to maintain the curved shape.

Now mark button positions on the back hessian using tailor's chalk. It is advisable initially to press tacks into the weave of the hessian to experiment with the visual effect of your proposed button positions. Sizes of diamond shapes will be approximately 16.5–17.5 cm ($6\frac{1}{2}$–7 in) × 12.5–14 cm (5–$5\frac{1}{2}$ in), depending upon the number of diamond shapes and size of the back. After establishing the positions for buttons with loose tacks, mark these on the back of the hessian with tailor's chalk – this is referred to as the groundwork.

Back covering should now be prepared calculating the size of covering needed using the following information. For full pleating between button positions, the distance between button markings on covering, both vertically and horizontally, must be greater than the distance between the button position markings on the ground hessian. For a suitable amount of fullness which will give ample pleating allow an additional fifth or 20% (approximately $\frac{3}{16}$ in to each 1 in) between buttons – that is, if groundwork marking is 16.5 cm ($6\frac{1}{2}$ in), covering should be marked 19.8 cm ($7\frac{1}{2}$–8 in) for length of diamond; if the groundwork width were 12.5 cm (5 in) the covering would be marked 15 cm ($5\frac{1}{2}$–6 in). Button positions should be marked upon reverse side of covering fabric, marking equally from each side of central vertical line (*figure* 50), horizontal lines of buttons being measured from the top line of fabric.

When assessing the size of fabric needed for the back of the chair, take the amount of extra fullness between buttons into account plus the amount of doming which must be given from the outside rows of buttons to the tacking point on outside of back (*figure* 49).

Now sew bridle ties for back filling into back hessian and onto the roll around sides and top. These ties should run diagonally, being positioned between rows of button markings. Cut lengths of twine of approximately 40 cm (16 in) equal to the number of buttons to be fixed in the back; pass each length through the hessian slightly to one side of a button marking and pass it back so that the twine straddles the button position on the hessian. The double length of twine should hang on the face of the hessian; it is advisable to make a light temporary knot in the two ends to keep them together.

The back should now be infilled with hair, deeply in the centre well, tapering off over the surface of the rolls. A minimum of three layers of skin wadding will be needed over the filling. Whilst laying the wadding over at twine positions, make a hole in the wadding to allow the twine to be drawn through; lay the wadding *very* loosely between button twines.

Starting with centre diamond buttons, thread both twines into buttoning needle and pass this twine and needle through fabric at marked position, pull one twine out from needle eye and pass the remaining twine through the tuft at base of button (or wire loop, if applicable). Form a slip knot with the two twines but, before tightening the knot, tuck a small folded piece of waste material into the twine tie at the back of the hessian. Known as a butterfly, this prevents the twine loop from being pulled through the hessian (*figure* 51). The slip knot should be eased partially tight temporarily whilst you tie in all the buttons. Set the pleating with a flat blunt tool, such as the end of an upholsterer's regulator, or even the flat handle of a spoon. Pleats should be set from the extreme outside buttons straight to outside of frame, well temporary tacked; folds of *all* pleating should be facing down towards the seat.

With all buttons in position and pleating set, ease slip knots down as tightly as possible to accentuate the concave shape of the back and tie them off securely (as in *figure* 51) with ends of twines cut off and tucked under edges of buttons. Covering should now be tacked home around edges of outside back.

Tack reinforcing lining hessian over outside back area with wadding over. Pin outside back covering into position and finally slipstitch around sides and top; tack the covering under bottom member, finishing by tacking a bottoming over the underside webbing approximately 1 cm ($\frac{1}{2}$ in) in from each edge.

Stick gimp or braid around the base of the chair.

III *Easy chairs and settees*

There are probably far more styles of easy chairs and settees than any other type of domestic furniture. Manufacturers of modern upholstered suites have always seemed more fashion conscious than those in any other section of the furniture trade and have felt the need to re-model most of their production ranges annually. Therefore, over the years with the continuous production of new styles and more efficient modern production, one seldom visits two homes to see the same upholstered suite in both. In a book such as this, it would be impossible to cover every possible modern style which readers may have in their homes.

There are, however, a number of basic methods of construction and basic use of materials which could be common to several styles of contemporary suites. By the selection and inclusion of a relatively small number of styles and methods of make up and materials required, readers may well be able to gain the information needed to repair or restore a particular upholstered item with which they may be concerned.

There is a much narrower field, however, with traditionally upholstered pieces – styles, construction details and materials are generally more standard. When stripping down dilapidated or antique upholstery, construction methods and materials will appear very similar.

Admittedly, the traditional style of upholstery using coil springing and loose natural fillings, which need to be stitched into rolls to make firm edges, is more time consuming. There is, however, satisfaction in being able to manage, shape and produce a work of *craft*, particularly if you work on it at home with no limits on production time.

52. Traditionally upholstered three-seater settee

TRADITIONAL STYLE UPHOLSTERY

As an introduction to this section, figure 52 shows a three-seater 2 m (6 ft 6 in) length settee upholstered luxuriously. The upholstery has been cut through to demonstrate the basic construction of all parts and materials used. This particular style was upholstered with a full seat, to avoid needing seat cushions, with an independent sprung edge and coil sprung arms.

This example of traditional upholstering is of the highest standard of craftsmanship using the best materials and would withstand many years of continuous wear far better than current productions using foam. However, you must consider the difference in costs between the mass-produced and hand-made settee.

Estimated quantitites of materials for complete upholstery (*figure* 52)

	Easy chair	Two seat settee	Three-seat settee
Webbing	25.0 m (28 yd)	33.0 m (36 yd)	40.0 m (44 yd)
Hessian springing quality	1.25 m ($1\frac{1}{3}$ yd)	1.83 m ($2\frac{1}{3}$ yd)	2.50 m ($2\frac{3}{4}$ yd)
Hessian 2nd quality	1.0 m (1 yd)	1.40 m ($1\frac{1}{2}$ yd)	2.06 m ($2\frac{1}{4}$ yd)
Spring 28 cm (11 in) × 9 swg (seat)	9	18	27
Springs 15 cm (6 in) × 10 swg (spring edge)	4	9	12
Springs 15 cm (6 in) × 12 swg (back)	6	12	18
Springs 15 cm (6 in) × 10 swg (back)	3	6	9
Springs 15 cm (6 in) × 12 swg (arms)	8	8	8
Fibre, 1st stuffing	5 kg (11 lb)	6.80 kg (15 lb)	9.0 kg (20 lb)
Hair, 2nd stuffing	3.75 kg ($8\frac{1}{2}$ lb)	5.50 kg (12 lb)	6.80 kg (15 lb)
Scrim 1.83 m (2 yd) width	1.83 m (2 yd)	2.75 m (3 yd)	3.20 m ($3\frac{1}{2}$ yd)
Calico undercover (1.83 m (2 yd) width)	1.83 m (2 yd)	2.75 m (3 yd)	3.20 m ($3\frac{1}{2}$ yd)
Bottoming 1.83 m (2 yd) width	0.76 m × 0.76 m (2 ft 6in × 2ft 6in)	0.76 m (2 ft 6 in)	2.13 m × 0.91 m ($2\frac{1}{3}$ yd × 1 yd)
Spring edge cane	1 m (3 ft 0 in)	2 m (6 ft 0 in)	2.75 m (9 ft 0 in)
Covering	4.12 m ($4\frac{1}{2}$ yd)	6.25 m (6.5–6 yd)	7.56 m ($8\frac{1}{3}$ yd)
Upholstery trimming cord	6.0 m ($6\frac{1}{2}$ yd)	7.60 m ($8\frac{1}{3}$ yd)	8.50 m ($9\frac{2}{3}$ yd)

Tacks—16 mm ($\frac{5}{8}$ in), 13 mm ($\frac{1}{2}$ in), 10 mm ($\frac{3}{8}$ in)
Laid cord or nylon cord—1 cop
Twine—1 cop
Linen slipping thread
Skin wadding

TOOLS

> Upholsterer's hammer
> Webbing stretching tool
> Ripping chisel and mallet, or substitute
> Scissors
> Spring needle or large circular needle 15 cm (6 in)
> Small circular needle 7.5 cm (3 in)
> 20–5 cm (8–10 in) long stitching needle
> 35 cm (14 in) long needle
> Upholsterer's regulator
> Upholsterer's skewers
> Sewing machine

Estimated quantities of materials needed for an easy chair and two or three-seater settees are given here. Should you be intending to totally re-upholster or partly upholster similar work, use the figures as a guide.

Cover cutting plans with approximate cutting sizes as a guide for an easy chair, two or three-seater settee as shown in figures 53–54. Although these are shown as separate plans, there could be a slight saving in total quantity if two chairs and a settee were cut simultaneously. Changing the 'full seat' version to accommodate seat cushions would require an additional quantity of covering fabric; shorter springs would also be needed in the seat 'well'.

Upholstering

I intend to describe construction for this traditionally upholstered style of chair in as great a detail as possible, bearing in mind that a settee is just an extension of an easy chair with a wider seat span. Numbers for webs and springing will refer to the easy chair upholstery.

Seat

Note that the seat is webbed with linen webbing, tacked to top surface of base members. This is due to the exceptional height of seat springs. To avoid webbing chaffing on inner edges of the rails, a length of webbing is fixed along all corner edges where the webbing would bear down upon it.

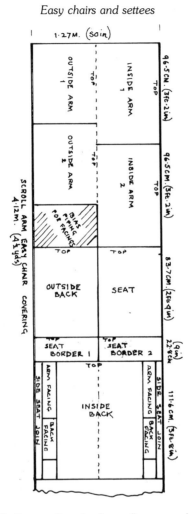

53. Cover cutting plan for scroll arm easy chair

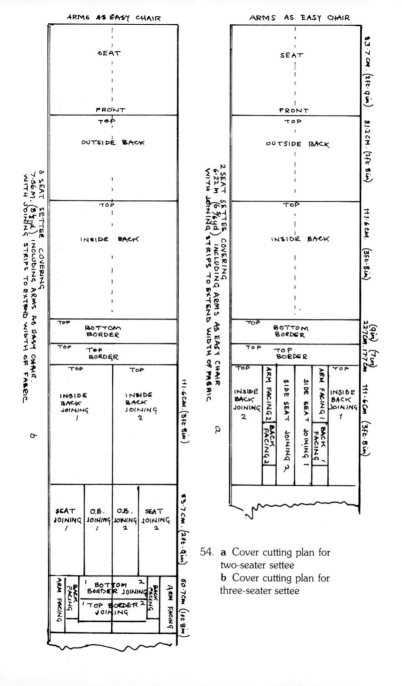

54. **a** Cover cutting plan for
two-seater settee
b Cover cutting plan for
three-seater settee

55. Additional reinforcing webbing for settee seat

Interlace and tension five strands of web across with six front to back as in figures 31–3. Use 16 mm ($\frac{5}{8}$ in) improved tacks.

Figure 55 shows how older slack webbing can be reinforced by tacking and tensioning new webbing over – this is provided that the main seat upholstery is in sound condition and does not need completely stripping.

Before sewing the springs to the webbing, line the inside arms with second quality hessian; first tack two supporting webs on bottom and top arm rails and then tack the hessian along the arm stay rail and along the top arm.

It is necessary when using exceptionally tall springs to 'double' lash – i.e. put an additional line of cord through centre coils before lashing the top coils (*figure* 56a). Fix shorter springs to the front spring edge member using 'U' wire staples or a length of web tacked over the bottom coil (*figure* 56b).

Cut a suitable length of flexible upholstery cane and shape it as in figure 57; tie it firmly along front of edge springs after tying springs to prevent any forward movement. The flexible spring edge should be kept independent

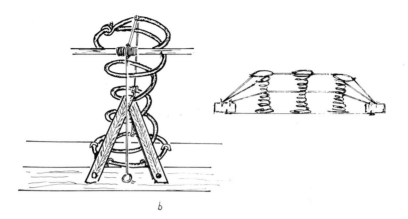

b

56. **a** Additional lashing through centre of seat **b** fixing of front edge springs

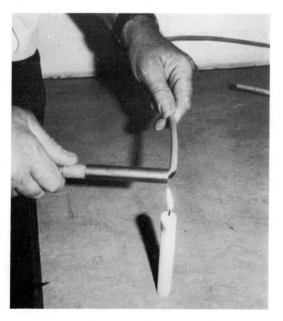

57. Bending of front spring edge cane

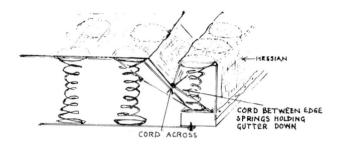

58. Forming the gutter at rear of spring edge

of the main springing by forming a 'gutter' when the hessian is fixed in position as shown in figure 58. Springs are sewn by their top coils (*figure* 59) and the hessian is sewn along the cane along front edge. First quality hessian for springs should be used. Tuck stuffing into the gutter and put first stuffing onto the spring hessian. Draw scrim over filling and pin it with skewers to front edge (*figure* 60). Stuffing ties are

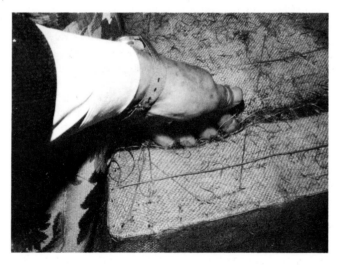

59. Tucking filling into the gutter

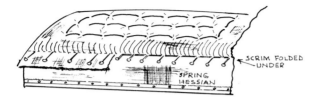

60. Use of skewers to pin out scrim on spring edge

run through as in figures 37–8, after which the scrim is sewn folded under to the hessian along cane line. Form a blind stitch and roll stitch along the edge. Apply hair second stuffing under bridle ties with the undercovering calico over and sew this along the front edge also.

Arms

Position 12 gauge arm springs along the top arm members and staple with 'U' wire staples. Tension webbing across top coils tacked on front and back; each side of the springs should be anchored with twine to prevent lateral movement and sewn to webbing also. Tack hessian only loosely over arm springs.

Apply filling fibre lightly to the shape of arms. These have a roll on front-facing formed by tacking scrim on bevelled edge around front of arm and finished with a blind and roll stitch, stitched with a 20 cm (8 in) long needle. A large roll is also made along the outside of the arm to give a 'roll over' effect. Two rows of stuffing ties are run through the scrim on inside of arm through to lining hessian. Apply second stuffing and undercover, tacking them under the front roll facing and under roll along the outside.

At this stage, top cover the arms and seat with wadding under the covering. Covering may need additional strips joined along each side of seat back and outside back. This is allowed for in the cutting plans.

Back

The back is webbed with 3 vertical × 4 horizontal webs, the two lower webs being placed close together to take the heavier gauge bottom row of springs. The two upper rows of springs are light 12 swg and the lower row is 10 swg. Back springs are lashed as in figure 52 and covered with spring quality hessian; top coils of springs are sewn to the hessian. A firm filled pad should be formed across top of back made with a strip of hessian, tacked on front edge of top member, filled with fibre and then tacked on the back edge.

The hessian again has bridle ties sewn into place with fibre fairly lightly applied under, scrim covering with ample stuffing ties through to prevent downwards movement of filling, and side back facings treated as the front arm facings with roll overhanging.

The back is second stuffed, with undercover followed by wadding and top covering. Outside arms and backs are lined with second quality reinforcing hessian being back tacked across top lines, i.e. under roll of the arm and under roll of the back, finishing on underside of frame.

There should be a double border finish to the front. The top border should be pinned to position, immediately under seat roll, and padded and tacked to spring edge rail. The lower border should be back tacked along the spring edge rail to cover tacking of bottom line of upper border. The lower border should be slightly wider than the one above; this should be also padded and finally tacked on the underside of the frame.

Pin the front arm and back facing coverings to the shape of facing with slight padding under and then slipstitch with a decorative upholstery cord sewn around the facing lines, under the seat edge and between the two borders. Tack a bottoming neatly on the underside using a second quality hessian or, alternatively, a dark coloured lining. Hessian may be used for extension flys beyond the sight lines at sides of seat, bottom of arms and back to reduce the cutting sizes of fabric.

Cushion seat

A cushion seat version of this particular style of traditional upholstery would necessitate introducing shorter length springs in the well and front edge of the seat – i.e. these should be 23 cm (9 in) with 10 cm (4 in) along front edge.

Apply filling spread thinner over the spring hessian than for a full seat and as flat as possible with just sufficient to insulate the springs; make the front roll less bold and stitch it in the same manner as the full seat.

To ensure that the seat cushions have a flat base to rest upon and to avoid a gap along the front below the cushion edges, form a 'lip' of approximately 12.5–15.0 cm (5–6 in) width and hold it down with twine sewn through the seat scrim.

An economy in covering fabric may be made if desired by using a matching lining beyond the back of the lip to back of the seat (*figure* 61). This will enable an appreciable saving in covering fabric on a suite as front borders of the cushion seat would consequently be narrower.

61. 'Lip' and 'platform' on cushion seat surface

Making the seat cushions

Fill seat cushions to complement the cushioned version of
the traditional chairs and settees in the previous section with
feathers or feathers and down; this, of course, is more
expensive and more time-consuming than making foam
cushions.

Poultry feathers (the less cheaper of the two) often
have rather thick quills making a coarse filling if used solely;
down, however, which consists of the light, fluffy under-
feathers of water fowl, has no quills and is luxurious. A
100% filling of down would be exorbitantly expensive, so
mixtures of feathers and down are generally used, the cost
depending upon the percentage of mixture. Most mixtures
are generally satisfactory for making seat cushions and are
hardwearing.

A feather and down filling needs to be encased
within an inner down-proof case made from cambric – a
closely woven, waxed cotton material that resists penetra-
tion of feather quills through to the outer covering. One side
only is waxed and this should be made up as the inner face.
The inner case should be machine edge stitched – i.e. both
edges folded in and machined on the extreme edge with a
small stitch using good quality cotton thread. The make up
of the inner case is shown in figure 62 with walls machined
to the top and lower panels to form separate compartments
in the cushion case. Stuff each of these to contain a share of
filling, which should remain in place throughout the life of
the cushion. The inner case should be cut 2.0 cm ($\frac{3}{4}$ in)
oversize on all sides to ensure that it fills the outer covering
well. Borders also should be cut 1 cm ($\frac{1}{2}$ in) oversize and one
end of each compartment should be left unstitched to allow
filling to be inserted. The cushion should then be hand sewn
or machined after filling.

Cushion cover cutting

Fitted cushions should be as accurately fitting as possible,
both in depth (front to back) and width without excessive
overhang at front and with a snug fit between arms, without
being over tight. Particular care should be taken in fitting

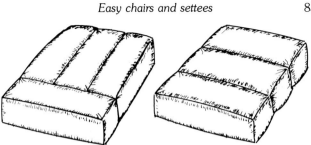

62. Make up of interior cases for feather cushions

seat and back cushions to settees with two or three or more cushions across the width so that they are not too tight; this would cause them to ride up when sat upon.

The initial stage in cushion making is to cut out a template from stout paper to the finished size following shape of bottom back to front edge and also following arm shape along sides. If you are cutting cushions for a settee cut two or three templates, dividing the width across the seat equally. Ignore any projections at side of end cushions when dividing.

If ruching is to be used as trimming around cushions, no allowance need be made on top and bottom panels for machining. This will enable the finished cushion to show off the projecting ruche nicely and avoid it being crushed between cushion and arms. If piping is to be used, make an allowance of 1 cm ($\frac{3}{8}$ in) on all sides of the template for machining. Cut piping on the bias (diagram 44 and 53).

When cutting covering for cushion, lay it out on a smooth table with full width of the covering folded down half width line, pin out template on surface of covering, and cut around it with sharp scissors, not forgetting seaming allowance if piped. (In mass production, a number of cushins would be cut simultaneously with electric cutting knife.)

Cutting top and bottom panels for a domed foam cushion, allow for the domed surface shape in addition to the normal seaming allowance (*figure* 63): instead of the outer lines of the panels being cut straight they should be

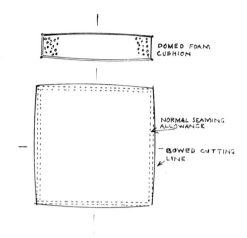

63. Cutting of domed cushion cover panel

convex, tapering off to normal seaming at extreme ends. This will avoid the rise in the centre of cushion distorting its outer lines. This is not necessary with feather and down cushions.

MODERN UPHOLSTERY: FOAM AND FABRICS

Foam cushions

So often foam cushions are a disappointment to many owners of relatively new modern upholstered suites. Many foam interiors flatten out with a loss of depth and resiliency quite quickly whilst the remainder of the suite is in a satisfactory condition. Unfortunately, the offending cushions tend to be continually used until the wear is reflected in the seat upholstery below, eventually resulting in the suite having to be disposed of.

It is quite easy to renew foam cushion interiors, providing, of course, the outer covering is in satisfactory, sound condition. Cushion covers normally have an opening at the rear – if zipped this usually is in the centre of back border, if sewn a row of slipstitching will be across one of the rear edges. When this stitching is cut through, you can remove the unserviceable interior.

It is essential that a suitable foam is purchased as replacement. Foam for seating purposes should be a good, firm quality, high resistant foam with small cellular construction and the right thickness, preferably 10 cm (4 in) depth. Foam intended for back cushions may be less firm and possibly thinner, perhaps 7.5 cm (3 in).

Two types of foam are available for cushion making: polyether (plastic) foam and latex (natural rubber) foam. Polyether is cheaper and readily available from upholstery sundries shops, D.I.Y. and most camping shops. It may be purchased pre-cut to standard cushion sizes or bought in sheet form. It is often difficult to get the pre-cut size to your requirements. Although foam is professionally cut with an electric cutting knife, it can be successfully cut at home using a domestic broad-bladed bread or carving knife.

Mark the size of foam to be cut, placing a template on the surface of the foam, with a thick point felt-tip pen. When cutting, hold foam with cutting line over edge of table (it is better to have help with this operation); with firm, *upright* strokes cut to the outside of the marked line. Ensure the cutting is perfectly upright. The foam should be fractionally over-size, i.e. 6 mm ($\frac{1}{4}$ in) on each cut line. Any excessive over-cutting will cause the foam to 'belly up' when forced into the cushion cover.

Latex foam is now produced mainly as 'pincore' sheet for cushion making and other uses as opposed to cavity sheet (*figure* 64), which was generally used some

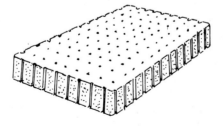

64. Pincore Latex foam

years earlier. A range of standard sized, moulded domed cushions made from two moulded half shapes taped together around centre borders are produced and are a good buy, superior to polyether foam in resiliency and ageing properties. These are not so readily available as polyether cut sizes but can generally be obtained from dealers specialising in upholstering sundries.

A 10 cm (4 in) cushion cut from pincore sheet produces flat undomed surfaces. To make a domed cushion two 5 cm (2 in) thicknesses should be used with a 2.5 cm (1 in) piece sandwiched in centre with edges tapered, outside edges of thicker foam being taped using adhesive and strips of lining or calico.

When cutting latex with a domestic knife, it is easier to cut it if the knife is dipped in water beforehand; this will lubricate the knife and prevent the gripping action of the latex.

A more luxurious foam cushion can be made by wrapping one or two thicknesses of Terylene 'fibre-fill' around the foam. The interior needs cutting a little undersize if this is to be done. Fibre-fill in sheet form can be purchased by the metre × 69 cm (2 ft 3 in) width from a number of fabric stores or upholstery sundries shops.

Fabric

Fabric used for upholstery covering should be more sturdy than that generally used for curtaining purposes. A number of departmental stores offer fabrics of different kinds at low cost for upholstering, but you should guard against purchasing lightweight fabric with loose weave and no body. This type of fabric would give unsatisfactory wear in view of the harsh treatment that a covered piece of upholstery is subjected to generally, not only from sitting but from idle fingers picking at and abrading the material. An inferior fabric will also soil more quickly.

Machining of fabric

Making up cushions and general machining of upholstery fabric calls for a fairly sturdy sewing machine. On occasions two, three or four (sometimes more) thicknesses of fabric have to be accommodated under the pressure foot and be guided around shapes and corners. Unfortunately, a number of lighter, modern domestic machines would not be able to feed this thickness of material through nor would the machine needle have the power to penetrate such thickness. It is wise to experiment with some sample lines and thicknesses initially before deciding to undertake what is, in fact, a difficult task with an unsuitable machine.

When making up a piped or ruched cushion case, it is better to sew the trimming to the main top and bottom panels first and then machine the borders on over the trimming flanges. Join borders at corners of cushions or centre a full width of border on the front, machine down the sides, and then add a further length of border to complete the circuit.

Using leather and simulated leather

An upholstered item covered in leather gives a luxurious appearance and a feeling of achievement. Unfortunately, the cost of leather for upholstery covering purposes is very high compared with most fabrics and, of course, is rather more difficult to manipulate.

Leather (cowhide) is sold by the square metre or square foot and only supplied by the well-stocked upholstery sundriesman or the currier (processor of cowhides). The size of a hide varies, an average skin being about 4.65 m^2 (50 sq ft), some skins being larger or smaller and supplied in many colours.

In general, the smallest quantity that is offered for sale is half a skin cut down the length (back bone) from neck to butt. Every cm^2 is charged for, which incurs an amount of wastage for unusable leather which must be accepted, leather being a natural product. However, it is possible that a small offcut of a size to fit a particular small project may be purchased from a manufacturer to clear his store of remnants.

Leather has different characteristics to fabric and needs more care when being used – it is particularly prone to damage by tacks and easily scratched by bad handling. It tends to split at cuts around arm and leg stiles rather more than fabric so great care is needed for this operation.

A heavier-than-normal sewing machine is needed for leather sewing and a larger stitch length should be used than that for fabric. It is necessary to cut templates for all parts to be cut from the skin so they may be laid upon the leather and moved around. This ensures maximum value with least waste.

Simulated leather – i.e. P.V.C., expanded vinyl or polyurethane coated materials to give that leather appearance – are supplied in lineal measures (metre/yard) and are more economical than natural leather because there is no more wastage than using fabric.

Modern leather and simulated leathers have excellent softness and are ideal for using over foam filling. In most cases they need laying over the foam only rather loosely without any tensioning so as not to distort the soft foam interior.

MODERN UPHOLSTERY: DEALING WITH DEFECTS

Figures 65 and 66 show a typical modern upholstered settee and easy chair with foam filled cushions with a wrap of fibre-fill to simulate feather cushions. Back and arms are upholstered with foam filling, 5 cm (2 in) rubber webbing supports seat cushions and the back is fitted with lengths of sinuous (serpentine) springing.

Covering on the arms is 'capped on', i.e. piped each side of the arm border, the whole arm being in one piece. Other styles of arms with simple methods of upholstery, together with other methods of seat upholstery and springing are shown in figure 67; these could well be an alternative to what is shown in figures 65–66.

After a number of years of continuous hard use, a variety of defects could in a style such as this present themselves causing the owner to consider remedial action.

A number of possible faults which generally occur are listed here, followed by suggested action:

65. Covered easy chair with 'capped on' arms

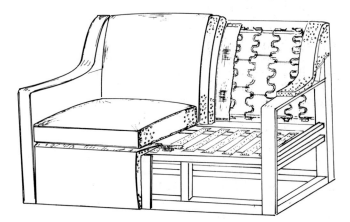

66. Cut-through section of upholstered settee

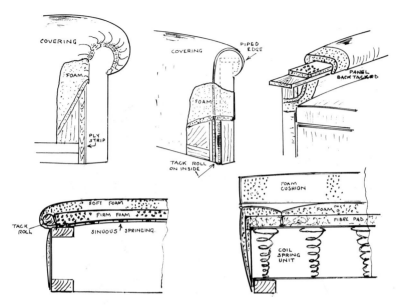

67. Examples of alternative methods of arm and seat upholstery

(1) Covering in need of replacement owing to soiling and wear.
(2) Loss of depth and resiliency of seat cushion foam.
(3) Rubber webbing of seat overstretches, perishes and generally becomes unserviceable.
(4) Foam on front edge disintegrates.
(5) Foam on back disintegrates allowing springs to be felt.
(6) Noisy back springs.
(7) Loose frame joint.
(8) If coil spring seat unit, springs buckle or break, making a noisy unit.
(9) If tension sprung seat, overstretching of springs or broken ends occurs.
(10) If serpentine or sinuous sprung seat, a clip breaks as the spring disengages from it or a broken nail.

Stripping covering

Release as much original covering as possible carefully from the staples or tacks holding it to the frame in one operation. It is not always prudent to remove totally all the covering; instead leave one or two tacks or staples holding the material to prevent the filling beneath moving too much.

Should the original covering have an amount of shaping, i.e. as arms in figure 65, this covering if removed carefully may be used as a cutting pattern or template when stitching is removed and the arm covering taken to pieces. If the old covering is used as cutting pattern, it is essential that when laid over the new fabric to be cut, the weave of the fabrics coincide and are at the right angle. It is advisable to pin it out securely on the cutting surface.

Defect 1: recovering

Figure 68 shows the plans for economic cutting of covering material using 127 cm (50 in) width of fabric.

If it is impossible to use the original old covering as cutting patterns, stout paper templates should be cut to the outside arm shape including the foam thickness. The template should reach to the base of the frame plus an amount equal to that needed for tacking covering to below frame.

Whilst the inside arm shape is identical for the top section, draw a line on the template from front to back at a position where the bottom edge of the inside arm stay rail is plus an amount to reach under the rail and tack on the outside face (side away from seat). This line should be the extent in depth of the inside arm and covering cut only to that point – cutting to the same depth as the outside arm would be a waste.

After rough cutting the pieces of cover for the arm panels they should be paired, i.e. two inside and two outside pieces faced together and laid upon the cutting table smoothly with the template laid over, pinned down securely to prevent movement whilst cutting, with the inner arms shorter than the outer as explained earlier. The four panels may then be cut simultaneously, all to precisely the same

TOOLS

Hammer or stapling tool
Scissors
Ripping chisel and mallet or substitute
Spatular for adhesive
Sewing machine

MATERIALS

	Easy chair	2-seat settee
Rubber webbing × 5 cm (2 in)	3.35 m ($3\frac{2}{3}$ yd)	7.32 m (8 yd)
Linen webbing	1.0 m (1 yd)	2.0 m (2 yd)
Hessian	1.40 m × 1.83 m width ($1\frac{1}{2}$ yd × 2 yd)	1.83 m × 1.83 m width (2 yd × 2 yd)
Foam (back)	0.61 m × 0.76 m × 5 cm (2 ft × 2 ft 6 in × 2 in)	1.22 m × 0.76 m × 5 cm (4 ft × 2 ft 6 in × 2 in)
Foam (seat)	0.61 m × 0.46 m × 2.5 cm (2 ft × 1 ft 6 in × 1 in)	1.22 m × 0.46 m × 2.5 cm (4 ft × 1 ft 6 in × 1 in)
Foam (arms)	2 m × 1.35 m × 1.5 cm (6 ft × 4 ft 6 in × $\frac{1}{2}$in)	As easy chair
Foam (arm borders)	1.22 m × 0.20 m × 2.5 cm (4 ft × 8 in × 1 in)	As easy chair
Foam (cushions)	0.51 m × 0.61 m × 10 cm (1 ft 8 in × 2 ft × 4 in)	2 as easy chair size
Back springs	5 lengths of sinuous spring or rubber webbing	12 lengths
Terylene fibre-fill	2 m (2 yd)	4 m (4 yd)
Covering	4.17 m ($4\frac{2}{3}$ yd)	6.0 m ($6\frac{2}{3}$ yd)
Cord		
Linen thread		
Tacks	13 mm ($\frac{1}{2}$ in), 10 mm ($\frac{3}{8}$ in)	
Adhesive		

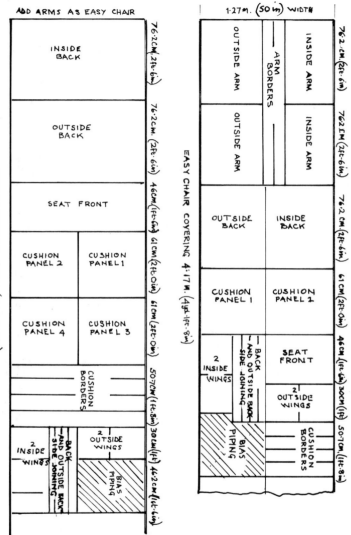

ADD ARMS AS EASY CHAIR

SETTEE COVERING 5·9 sq m (6 yd·1ft·8 in)

1·27 m (50 in) WIDTH

EASY CHAIR COVERING 4·17 m (4 yd·1ft·8 in)

Settee plan:

INSIDE BACK — 76·2 cm (2ft·6 in)

OUTSIDE BACK — 76·2 cm (2ft·6 in)

SEAT FRONT — 46 cm (1ft·6 in)

CUSHION PANEL 2 | CUSHION PANEL 1 — 61 cm (2ft·0 in)

CUSHION PANEL 4 | CUSHION PANEL 3 — 61 cm (2ft·0 in)

CUSHION BORDERS — 50·7 cm (1ft·8 in)

2 INSIDE WINGS | BACK AND OUTSIDE BACK SIDE JOINING | OUTSIDE WINGS | BIAS PIPING | 2 — 30 cm (1ft) / 46·2 cm (1ft·6 in)

Easy chair plan:

OUTSIDE ARM | ARM BORDERS | INSIDE ARM — 76·2 cm (2ft·6 in)

OUTSIDE ARM | INSIDE ARM — 76·2 cm (2ft·6 in)

OUTSIDE BACK | INSIDE BACK — 76·2 cm (2ft·6 in)

CUSHION PANEL 1 | CUSHION PANEL 2 — 61 cm (2ft·0 in)

2 INSIDE WINGS | BACK AND OUTSIDE BACK SIDE JOINING | SEAT FRONT — 46 cm (1ft·6 in)

2 OUTSIDE WINGS

BIAS PIPING | CUSHION BORDERS — 50·7 cm (1ft·8 in)

68. Cover cutting plan for easy chair and settee diagrams 65 and 66

outer shape not omitting seaming allowance. Should three pairs of arms be needed, the same process can be carried out for the remainder.

Cut borders for the total width of arm plus allowance for seaming each side. Make a 'vee' cut opposite on both sides of each border at the top corner positions. This will ensure that when they are sewn together corners will be square on border and not out of position, which could easily happen if they were not marked.

First fix seat front covering into position over the rubber webbing which is tensioned from front to back. To hold the front covering into position, tension a length of linen webbing tightly across the surface of the rubber webbing (from side to side) with the back edge of the web 12.5–15.0 cm (5–6 in) from the front edge of the frame. Tuck front covering under this cross web and tack it along front seat member; lay foam over this web and front rail. Then draw over the tacked covering (as *figure* 13) and tack on underside of base member. The open space between seat and base rails should be lined with hessian, strong card or thin plywood.

After renewing arm foam if necessary, draw down the arm covers over foam on arms; tack the inside arms along outside of stay rail along bottom edge, and back, and along inside of back leg; and tack the outside arm along bottom member and back of back leg.

Lay back covering over back foam first by temporary tacking; finish off with tacking along outside top rail outside of bottom stay rail and tack sides on inside of back legs. Back tack the outside back along top of outside top rail, tack under base rail, pin out the sides, and finally slipstitch down the two side edges.

Line the inside and outside arms and outside backs with a second quality hessian to reinforce the covering.

If fabric is folded under when being tacked on the underside of the frame, a bottoming fabric need not be used.

Defect 2: renewing foam cushions

Foam measuring 10 cm (4 in) in depth, of high resistant seating quality, should be used for seat cushions for an easy chair or settee as illustrated. Moulded domed latex foam interiors, although the most expensive, are the best buy, providing suitable sizes are available.

Pincore latex foam (*figure* 64), a little less expensive than the moulded shape, can be cut to the required size and shape, has a good life expectancy and good resiliency. It is best to encase latex foam cushion interiors with a closely woven cotton calico or lining to prevent early deterioration. A loosely woven outer covering will allow strong light to filter through and shorten the life of the rubber interior.

Polyether foam is more readily available than latex at D.I.Y. stores etc., and is the least expensive with generally a variety of pre-cut sizes available; it is used in a high proportion of present day upholstered suites. A *good quality* polyether foam will give satisfactory performance over a number of years if a little care is taken in purchasing it. Before purchasing foam for renewing cushion interiors, test it to ensure that the foam is of good density, i.e. with minute cellular structure as opposed to the larger cells of poorer quality foam. Foam should have a firm resistance against compression – poorer qualities will loose height rapidly. It is wise to reject substandard foam or that which is too soft and not intended for seating.

If the required pre-cut size is not available, purchase the next larger size or, if cutting two or more interiors, obtain a sheet of the correct depth from which your sizes may be cut. Make a template to the seat size, mark around edges of the template using a felt-tip pen on to the foam and, using a broad-bladed bread or meat carving knife, cut around the outside of the drawn line so that the cut size is 6 mm ($\frac{1}{4}$ in) oversize on all sides. If laying the template adjacent to a pre-cut edge, allow that oversize along that edge also. This amount of oversize will give a suitable tension to the outer covering.

When using a wrap of Terylene fibre-fill over foam to enhance its softness, it is better to encase the complete interior, including the wrap, with cotton cheesecloth. Draw this around the exterior of the cushion filling, moulding it to size and shape; the cheescloth is then hand sewn. This is particularly important if covers have zips.

The original cushion cover, if it has no zip, should have a slipstitched join along one back edge. This stitching should be cut away and the old foam interior withdrawn. In inserting the new foam interior, it may be necessary to fold partially the foam to help insert it into the cover case. Pin the opening together and slipstitch it again.

Defect 3: replacing rubber webbing

In common with other forms of rubber, rubber webbing will deteriorate after several years of contant use, particularly if left open to a warm centrally heated atmosphere and bright light. When it deteriorates the webbing overstretches causing excessive deflection when you sit on it, resulting in uncomfortable, low sitting positions. Frequently, slack webbing will cause the metal fixing plate, if present, to slip out of its groove, or other metal fixing to come adrift. Consequently, it is essential to replace the webbing.

Figures 14 and 15 show rubber webbing being replaced on a fireside chair seat using tacks in one instance. Figure 20 shows steel plates being pressed onto the ends of strands of webbing; these are fitted into a groove in the seat frame member. The process of replacing rubber webbing on an easy chair or settee is a similar process to that shown.

Ensure that each strand is tensioned equally as described. Should strands be considerably longer than a fireside chair seat, as they probably would be, increase tension of the strands from $7\frac{1}{2}\%$ to 10% when fixing into position. It may be necessary to lift the front covering along the front of seat and possibly also the back to gain access to the ends of webbing. Also on some easy chairs there may be covering side strips which may have to be released.

Defect 4: front edge foam replacement

If seat cushion foam collapses, the front edge foam suffers and will often break up and fall from its position on the front rail. When you renew cushion foam also attend to this front edge foam.

Lift the covering along front of seat – this is generally tacked or stapled onto the underside of base front member. Remove all old foam and replace it with a good depth of firm resistant foam.

Figure 13 shows foam being replaced on a front edge. Use adhesive along the front member if practical to ensure that the foam retains its position. Do not over tension the covering when re-tacking or stapling and allow the foam to maintain its full depth.

Defect 5: replacing back foam

Invariably the failure of back foam results from the chair or settee being put with its outside back adjacent to a radiator. This close constant heat will cause premature ageing and break down the foam, making the springing beneath protrude at various places and be felt through the covering.

To remove old foam and replace it with new, first completely take off the outside back covering. Remove: tacks or staples fixing the outside covering on the underside of the frame; stitching or gimp-pinning down sides of outside; and back tacking across the top of the back. Release the back covering along the top by removing tacks or staples that are down sides of back and bottom. In some instances, as in figures 65 and 66, the back section of the outside arms must be opened so you can remove tacks down the sides of the back.

Completely remove the back covering and old foam and replace foam positioned over the base hessian. Stick a strip of lining or calico across the top line of foam to act as a tacking flange – this should be tacked or stapled to the outer face of back rail. Now replace covering, ensuring cuts around stiles are positioned correctly and not showing loose yarns; then replace the remainder of covering.

Defect 6: noisy back springing

Generally, there are two basic reasons for noisy backs of modern easy chairs and settees and both may be attributed to springing.

69. Fixing of sinuous spring

Sinuous or serpentine springing is often one source of annoying creaking or squeaking. Each length of spring is attached to the timber frame by a thin metal clamp nailed to the frame member (*figure* 69); this holds one section of the last 'U' bend of the spring, forming a hinging action. When new the metal clamps have a lining within the jaws which insulates and prevents friction between the metal of the clamp and the wire spring and so should be silent when working.

After a number of years' use, however, or sometimes earlier if there is a faulty clamp, movement of one or more springs may cause an annoying squeak each time the spring is moved within the clamp.

To rectify this, lift up the upholstery around the area where you suspect the squeaking. Take out a nail holding the top jaw of the clamp and prize the jaw slightly open to release the end of the spring. Insert a small piece of fabric or small section of plastic or polythene sheet into the clamp and replace the spring, hammering down the top section of the clamp. Replace a new nail to secure it firmly, and replace the disturbed upholstery.

Should you find that after lifting the upholstery the back springing consists of single cone coil springs riveted to a steel lath or web, any noise from this could well come from one of the metal laths. One may have worked loose because the head of the nail has broken or perhaps a lath may have become buckled causing it to 'spring' each time it is used.

In this case take out the clout-nail holding the buckled lath and straighten and re-tension as tightly as possible the offending metal strip. If the replacement nail is hammered home at an angle away from the metal lath, it will tend to tighten it as it is hammered in the timber.

Defect 7: loose frame joints

Figure 7 shows flat steel plates suitable for screwing to the upholstery frame to reinforce unstable joints. Unfortunately, loose joints cannot be completely knocked apart on an easy chair or settee unless a major stripping of the upholstery takes place. The next best remedy, however, is to release the upholstery from around the faulty joint, to widen it as much as possible so that some fresh adhesive can be worked in, then close the joint as tightly as possible with the aid of a sash cramp if one can be fitted, and finally screw the steel plates in position.

One or two thicknesses of wadding laid over the plate, if it is on the outside of the frame, will insulate it and prevent its outline showing through the covering.

Defect 8: faulty coil spring seat unit

Many fully upholstered deeply sprung seats of easy chairs and settees similar to those illustrated are fitted with a 'spring' unit (*figure 70*). This has a number of single cone springs with their bases riveted to a metal web, with the top coils intertwined into a mesh platform on which hessian and filling is applied. A less expensive version has top coils clipped together with metal straps. (There are a number of other types.) The construction of a unit sprung seat is more economical to produce than a hand-sprung seat with individual springs and webbing.

A good spring unit fitted in a seat will give satisfactory wear over many years, but faults may develop mostly through misuse, i.e. if someone stands on it to reach a high shelf with their weight on side or corner springs, or, if children jump on it.

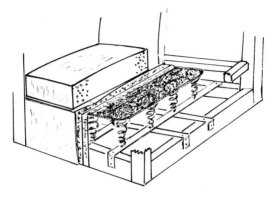

70. Easy chair seat upholstered with spring unit

A typical fault that develops is for one or two of the springs to weaken or buckle, particularly along the side or corner of the seat, causing the sitter to be thrown to one side as he sits down. Abnormal weight on one or two of the springs only will often snap the spring wire, causing the loss of two or three coils of a spring, and this will accentuate the buckling of some of the remaining springs.

A further problem frequently with an ageing unit spring within a seat is noise. When you shift position, a metallic grinding noise may be heard from the seat. This is caused by the coils of springs and the mesh platform abrading together. When manufactured, spring units are frequently coated with black lacquer paint which serves as an anti-rust and anti-noise treatment and some are coated with a thin film of wax. Eventually, however, these treatments wear away.

Unfortunately, it is not generally possible for you to obtain replacement springs units or to get the correct size unit unless you are lucky enough to be near a good upholstery shop or warehouse with a comprehensive stock. Very rarely is it possible to repair satisfactorily a damaged unit. In fact, it is not wise to do so as a straightened buckled spring will invariably return to its buckled state within a short time.

The best thing to do with a damaged seat spring unit is to completely strip the seat upholstery down, remove the unit and replace it with woven webbing and normal double cone springs 10 swg, carrying out the procedure described on pp. 32–42. The new double cone springs should be a little higher than the original size unit spring by 5 cm (2 in). This will counteract loss of height when you lash it with cord.

Defect 9: overstretched or unserviceable tension springing

The use of tension springing for seat suspension systems for easy chairs and settees similar to those illustrated here has over recent years declined and been superseded by resilient rubber webbing. However, there are many small up-holstered suites which have been constructed using tension springing to support seating cushions with overstretched and faulty springing.

Easy chairs normally have the lengths of spring hooked onto plates screwed to side members of the seat with the springs running side to side; settees mostly have their plates scewed to front and back members so the springs run front to back. On occasions there is a centre timber member down the centre of the settee seat to which plates are screwed and, in which case, the spring lengths run from side to side as the easy chair springing.

Pages 14–22 and figures 14, 15 and 20 describe the advantages and show the method of replacing the original tension springing with rubber webbing if replacement springs are unobtainable. You will find that a superior seat will result from the change to rubber webbing. The new strands of rubber webbing should be applied in the same direction as the lengths of spring were positioned – this would normally be across the shorter span of seat.

Defect 10: faulty sinuous seat spring

Figure 66 shows this type of spring consisting of lengths of springing made from a continuous series of 'U' bends. Several upholstery spring manufacturers make similar forms with their own brand names which are not mentioned here.

This form of springing used for seat and back upholstery basically is very reliable, but occasionally one or two faults may develop with the springs which are not too difficult to put right.

It will be seen in figure 69 that the spring is held in place with a thin metal clamp, as indicated on page 98. The nail holding the upper jaw of the clamp may loose its head, allowing the spring wire to detach. When this happens, the length of springing will curl itself under and show below the seat; if a bottoming is tacked below the springs, a bulge will appear in the bottoming. The strands of sinuous springing will form themselves into an arc when released owing to the method of manufacture.

To reinstate a length of spring which has become detached, lift the upholstery along the front of the seat to get at the faulty spring position. With a length of stout cord form a loop with the two ends wrapped around the palm of your hand, catch one of the 'U' bends in the looped cord and tug it upwards. Guide the end section of the last 'U' into the clamp, hammer down the top leaf of the clamp and re-nail.

On occasions the metal clamp may fracture, i.e. the top leaf of the clamp will break off at the bend; this will also release the spring strand, which will then curl under. To rectify this remove the remaining part of the clamp and replace it with a short length of upholstery webbing tacks tightly wrapped around the end of the spring, tacking close to the wire using 16 mm ($\frac{5}{8}$ in) so it is held securely. It is wise to fold the webbing double for extra strength.

Before replacing upholstery along the front, check all the other clamps to ensure others are not on the verge of becoming detached.

IV *French period style upholstery*

Refurbishing French period style upholstery items needs far more care and precise workmanship than most other forms of re-upholstering. Invariably the framework of this style is much more fragile than the normal upholstery frame, often with highly decorative carvings and mouldings with gilt finish. Many pieces have decoration applied with Gesso (a mixture of plaster and glue), which is easily damaged by an accidental knock. This is very difficult to repair successfully unless you are experienced in that form of decoration.

Covering for the finer classes of these chairs and settees, etc., is often of fine silk fabric which poses problems with tacking, for example, tack ties in figure 71, especially if the silk is aged and needs replacing. Most of the covering is tacked into narrow rebates alongside the filling; consequently, there is a high risk of hitting the gilt or polished finish adjacent to the edge of rebate. An upholsterer's cabriole hammer (*diagram* 4) is a great aid when hammering tacks home against a polished edge.

Figure 72 shows an easy chair with covering of fine watered silk with piped finish to the feather cushion. A precaution which is worth observing when working on such a chair can be seen in figure 73: the legs of the chair are wrapped with a protective cover of paper or cloth and in this case corrugated paper is being used. Put this wrapping on before you start the work. If you leave it to later damage is sure to occur before you put it on. Having outlined some of

71. Showing 'tack ties' in silk covering of outside back

72. French-style easy chair covered in silk fabric

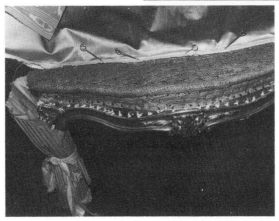

73. Sewing 'lip' covering across front of seat

the problems or difficulties to be faced, I hope these pre-cautions will not, however, deter you from refurbishing your favourite chair.

CARVER OR ELBOW DINING CHAIR (*figure* 74)

If upholstered true to style this chair seat should be top stuffed, i.e. upholstery should be applied to top of seat members without introducing springing. However, modern reproductions are often upholstered with seat springing using coil springs or even modern sinuous springing.

Should your example have a sprung seat and springs that need replacing, pages 32–42 will give you the appropriate information.

MATERIALS FOR A CARVED CHAIR TOP STUFFED
>Linen webbing—4.12 m ($4\frac{1}{2}$ yd)
>Hessian 1st quality—0.60 m × 0.90 m (2 ft × 3 ft)
>Upholsterer's scrim—1 m × 1.83 m (1 yd × 2 yd)
>Horsehair stuffing—1.81 kg (4 lb)
>Calico—0.60 m × 0.90 m (2 ft × 3 ft)
>Covering—0.76 m × 1.27 m width ($\frac{5}{6}$yd × 50 in width)
>Gimp trimming—3.66 m (4 yd)
>Extra if gimped around outside back—0.91 m (1 yd)
>Twine
>Tacks—13 mm ($\frac{1}{2}$ in), 10 mm ($\frac{3}{8}$ in)
>Adhesive
>Gimp pins—13 mm ($\frac{1}{2}$ in)

TOOLS
>Hammer, small-faced, and cabriole hammer if obtainable
>Scissors
>Ripping chisel and mallet
>Webbing tensioning tool
>Stitching needle 20/25 cm (8/10 in)
>Large circular or spring needle
>Upholsterer's regulator
>Spatular for adhesive

74. French-style carver chair

Stripping

Strip off gimp trimming; there will be gimp pins securing the gimp on the corners and these will sometimes be difficult to remove. Use a fine sharp ripping tool working away from the corners of the rebates, but don't let the tool slip. Remove covering and as much of the upholstery as needed in one stage.

If re-covering only and the outside back is tacked on the inside of the back frame, unfortunately you must remove the complete back.

Upholstering back and arm pads

It is more convenient to start work first on the back, then the arm pads and finally the seat. Panel backs vary regarding the method of outside back finish. In some cases the covering is tacked into a rebate on the outside of the frame, in which case it is positioned after the inside of the back is completed, or, as mentioned in the previous paragraph, you may have to tack it on the face of the back frame before you apply any webbing or hessian.

Tack one strand of webbing in each direction on the inside of the frame. If the outside back covering has first been tacked in position, lay two or three layers of sheet wadding over the bare covering to insulate the webbing to avoid any show-through or feel of the webbing. Tack hessian over the webbing using 10 mm ($\frac{3}{8}$ in) tacks. Whilst tacking around the back ensure that it is well supported so as not to overstrain the joints of the back.

When sewing bridle ties into the back hessian to hold filling in position, take care not to let the circular or spring needle penetrate the covering if it is immediately under the hessian. Amply temporary tack calico or lining under-covering over the back filling to ensure 'fullness' is worked out around the curved shape of the back. Tacking needs to be quite close at positions of the bias weave (*figure* 75). After laying two or three thicknesses of wadding over, treat the back covering in the same way, tacking with 10 mm ($\frac{3}{8}$ in) fine tacks. Hammer tacks gently home in a position where they will be covered by the trimming gimp.

Arm pads need a minimum of filling. Frequently if the chair is being refurbished, the arm pads need little attention other than re-covering, but it is wise to replace

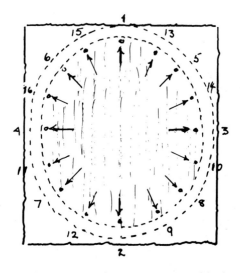

75. Sequence of temporary tacking covering on oval back to eliminate 'fullness'

fresh wadding over the calico undercover before putting on
the top covering.

Seat upholstery

Strands of webbing for a top stuffed seat should be tacked
on the top surface of seat members. A carver or elbow chair
needs 4×3 strands of linen webbing tacked with 13 mm
($\frac{1}{2}$ in) improved tacks with hessian over them. Re-rasp the
chamfer on seat frame edges to remove any roughness
caused by removing tacks from the original upholstery. This
will make it easier to place the new tacks when re-tacking
the scrim over the filling around the edge.

   If you wish to replace springing or to introduce
springing where there was none originally, webbing should
be placed on the underside of the seat members to allow
springs to be placed within the framework of the seat. The
application of bridle ties, filling, placing of scrim and stitching, second stuffing, under-covering, top covering and application of trimming gimp is as described on pages 56–61.

FRENCH STYLE SHOW-WOOD EASY CHAIR
(*figure* 72)

   French style easy chairs, as with similar style dining
chairs and occasional chairs, are also of very light construction with fragile frame and joints. They have a large amount
of show-wood usually heavily decorated with moulding and
carving which may have gilt or polish finish. Consequently,
these frames need infinite care when you handle them or
apply upholstery to avoid damage.

   Figure 72 shows a fairly common French style of
easy chair with a feather cushion to the seat, the seat being
top stuffed – that is, with no seat springing. A particular
feature of this form of upholstery is the outstanding upholstered back panel and, in the example shown, the arm
panels too. This type of panelled upholstery calls for skill in
stuffing and stitching the edges to preserve the shape of the
frame in the upholstery and to attain an even depth of panel

MATERIALS

Linen webbing—10.06 m (11 yd)

Hessian—0.60 m × 0.60 m (2 ft × 2 ft)

Scrim—1 m × 1.83 m (1 yd × 2 yd)

Hair filling—4.57 kg (9 lb)

Calico—1.14 m × 0.91 m width ($1\frac{1}{4}$ yd × 1 yd width)

Waxed cambric—1.30 m × 1.22 m width ($1\frac{1}{2}$ yd × 4 ft width)

Feathers—2 kg (4 lb)

Sheet wadding—1 roll

Covering—3.20 m ($3\frac{1}{2}$ yd) diagram 78

Trimming gimp—9.14 m (10 yd)

Tacks—16 mm ($\frac{5}{8}$ in), 13 mm ($\frac{1}{2}$ in), 10 mm ($\frac{3}{8}$ in)

Gimp pins—10 mm ($\frac{3}{8}$ in)

Twine

Piping cord

Adhesive

Tools as previous example

Sewing machine

edging throughout. A fine stitched edge is required using a large circular needle (15 cm (6 in)), rather than the long straight needle used for normal straight stitched edges.

Stripping upholstery

Although in an earlier section I advised you to upturn an item for the convenience of removing bottoming and covering around the base, it is better not to do this here as the top of the back is too delicate to withstand such treatment. Lay the chair on its back or with the arm pads resting on a table surface to keep the top of the back from the floor whilst you remove the bottoming. Carefully remove the gimp by lifting the gimp pins at corners and joins; take care to use the ripping tool away from moulding at corners.

If the outside back covering is affixed to the outside of the outer frame, it may not be necessary to strip completely the inside back and arm panels. Should the stitched edges around the back and arm panels appear to be sound and reasonably square after removing the old covering, with two or three thicknesses of new wadding over them you may need only to re-cover them.

The example in figure 72, however, shows the outside back tacked on the inner face of the back, which necessitates complete stripping of the back. Assuming complete re-upholstery is to be undertaken, the chair should be stripped to the basic framework.

Upholstery of back and arms

Outside back should be tacked into position on inner face of back using 10 mm ($\frac{3}{8}$ in) tacks, tacking clear of rebate. Note that in figure 71 horizontal lines are showing across the covering. These are tack ties caused by the covering being tensioned too tightly across the width, with insufficient tension being applied vertically as each tack is put in. If tensioning is not correct, each tack will cause a line to appear at the point of its insertion. In fact, the number of tacks used may be seen from these lines but with a little practice you can avoid this effect.

It is advisable to lay two or three thicknesses of wadding on the covering before applying webbing. The webbing should be hand tensioned only, thus avoiding possible damage to show-wood by using the web tensioner. Tack one vertical web from bottom back rail to top inside back member in each half. Pass three webs behind the vertical webs tensioning only lightly and tack them on face of side members – 13 mm ($\frac{1}{2}$ in) tacks may be used hammered in gently. Tack hessian over the webbing tensioning by hand vertically only without tension side to side. Two vertical webs are needed on the inside of each arm – these should also be lined with hessian.

Cut scrim for the back approximately 10 cm (4 in) larger than the outside line of the back, lay this over the back hessian, and temporary tack it to position around the rebate with weave straight in both directions.

With chalk or felt-tip pen draw a line 10 cm (4 in) in from the rebate edge, following the line of the back from top of arms all round the back. With a circular needle and twine, using a running stitch, sew along the drawn line fixing the scrim to the hessian, leaving a loose flange all around the back with centre scrim tight and flat on the hessian. Whilst doing this operation, ensure that the needle does *not* penetrate through the outside back cover – just pick up only the hessian with the needle point.

Sew bridle ties into the hessian, again taking care not to sew through the outer cover in the centre section and under the loose flange. Infill with stuffing around the sides under the loose flange and temporary tack scrim over filling with tacks into rebate. Using 10 mm ($\frac{3}{8}$ in) tacks, tack scrim folded *under* onto rebate (leave clearance from outer edge for width of gimping to be used). Try to obtain a wedge shape with the scrim and filling – the outer edge when stitched should be approximately 4 cm ($1\frac{1}{2}$ in) deep tapering thinly to the inner back. The stitched edge should be perpendicular or square from the rebate (*figure* 76).

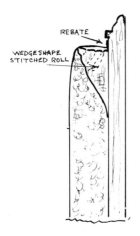

REBATE

WEDGE SHAPE
STITCHED ROLL

76. Wedge-shaped roll around edges of panel back

To stitch such an edge you need a large circular needle. To form the blind stitch insert the needle into the edge slightly above the tacking, drawing the twine through to the thinner part of the wedge shape; draw the twine out, reverse the needle and pass the point back through the same hole in the scrim. Draw it out through the side again so that the twine forms a loop within the scrim which may be drawn tight, pulling the filling forward to the edge. This operation is rather more complicated than using a straight needle which travels back and forth. The final top stitch should be a firm clean edge faithfully following the shape of the back.

Treat the arms similarly by forming a wedge of scrim and stitching with a well towards centre of arm. Stitching should be the same depth where it joins the back.

Fill the back with horsehair right up to the stitched edges, preserving the flat curving shape of the back. Then cover it with calico or lining, fold the edges under and pin around the extreme edge of the stitching. Under – cover the arms in the same way, and oversew pinned edges using a small circular needle and linen thread.

Temporary tack the inside back and arm covering into position so they may be fitted and cut accurately at rear of arm and base of back for machine joining with piped seam. After removal for machining, lay 2–3 thicknesses of sheet wadding smoothly over the under-covering and covering, which you then must replace accurately to align the piped seams equally on both sides. Tack home using 10 mm ($\frac{3}{8}$ in) fine tacks which should be placed fairly close together, tensioning the fabric *lengthwise* along the line of tacks. Do *not* pull the fabric tighter across at one point so that any one tack will cause a tack tie (*figure* 71). Place tacks to allow a good width for the gimp to bed down on flat. All this is best done before seat is installed.

At this stage a seat may be top webbed as is the example in figures 72–3 with seat cushion over. Alternatively, for a full seat (with no cushion) this should be webbed on the underside of the seat members to accommodate springs within the frame. Apply 5 × 4 strands of webbing in both instances, taking care when tensioning webbing to avoid damage to show-wood. If you are using springs 3 × 3 or 4 × 3 rows of springs will be necessary depending upon width of seat. A wider seat may need the four rows across width.

Normally 15 cm (6 in) or 18 cm (7 in) × 10 swg springs would be suitable for a full seat. If springs are introduced into a cushion seat, 12.5 cm (5 in) would be appropriate. Lash springs as shown in figure 34 and pages 35–7 tacking the hessian over; for the top webbed seat tack the hessian over the webbing.

Bridle ties and filling should be applied to both examples figure 73 shows three rows of stitching along the front edge – blind, roll and fine top stitch – with height of top stitching being 4 cm ($1\frac{1}{2}$ in) from edge of frame. This needs to be low to accommodate the cushion. Full seat version sprung seat stitching should be approximately 7.5–8 cm ($3–3\frac{1}{2}$ in) in height. First and second stuffings and processes are described on pages 35–42.

Figure 73 shows the method of attaining a flat seat suitable for the cushion to rest upon. A line of upholsterer's skewers holds the covering along a machined hem line between fabric of the lip and platform. This line is ready to be sewn with a long straight needle and twine running through the scrim, filling and base hessian using stitches approximately 2.5 cm (1 in) length. These are sewn across the full width of the seat forming a running line without knotting. When complete the width is sewn and the twine is eased down tightly to form an indentation between the lip and platform.

A thin filling of hair and wadding is applied over the seat platform and lip, the covering is drawn over and tacked home. This treatment is not necessary with the full seat version, this being fully stuffed with a slight doming to surface of the seat. Arm pads may be upholstered as in figure 77 with an emphasis on a slim, dainty finish.

Open area of outside arms should be lined with hessian with wadding over to smooth any irregularities; tack the covering with 10 mm ($\frac{3}{8}$ in) tacks.

77. Upholstery of arm pad

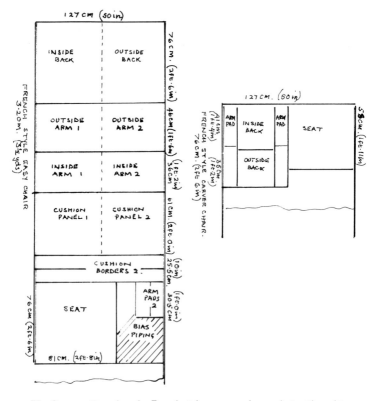

78. Cover cutting plans for French style carver and easy chair with cushion

Should the cushion need completely renewing, make an inner case from waxed cambric to contain the feathers as described on pages 82–3 and figure 62. First make a template to fit the seat area and shape. With the cambric folded double, laid upon a flat cutting surface, pin the template down securely and then cut around it allowing 2 cm ($\frac{3}{4}$ in) extra all around.

Use the template subsequently for cutting the outer covering for the cushion outer case allowing 1 cm ($\frac{3}{8}$ in) all round for seaming. Leave an opening at the rear when machining to insert the interior.

Now carefully apply gimp around all tacked edges of covering but, before attempting to use adhesive, put a protective sheet over the area of covering being worked upon. (If this precaution is not taken, a blob of adhesive is bound to drop on the covering.) Apply a neat bottoming fabric to the underside but do not upturn the chair and rest the weight on the top of the back.

GLOSSARY

Abrading   Wearing away by rubbing

Algerian fibre   Dyed grass used as first stuffing in upholstery

Alva   Dried seaweed used as upholstery filling during the Victorian period

Back tacking   A method of attaching covering to hide tacks

Bayonet needle   Long upholstery needle with triangular end

Bevel   Removal of sharp corner edge of timber rail (as chamfer)

Bias cutting   Cutting fabric diagonally across threads as 45°

Blind stitching   Stitching with twine to form loops within filling

Bottoming fabric   Material used to neaten the underside of upholstered items

Brace   Short piece of timber used to strengthen joints

Bridle ties   Loops of twine sewn into hessian to hold filling

Buckled spring   Upholstery spring with deformed coils (as crippled)

Butt   Rear end of a cowhide

Butterfly   Scrap of material used to prevent twine pulling through hessian

Cabriole hammer   Upholstering hammer with extra small face

Calico   Coarse cotton cloth used for undercovering of upholstered items

Cambric   Finely woven cotton fabric used to make feather cushion interior cases

Canvas   (Hessian) Coarse cloth made from jute fibre used to support upholstery filling

Cheesecloth Stretchable cotton fabric with knitted construction

Coir fibre Upholstery filling obtained from outer covering of coconut

Cotton felt Compressed cotton fibres formed into thick soft lap for upholstery filling

Cotton flocks Filling used during Victorian period from waste cotton fibres, also containing husk

Cotton shoddy Upholstery filling made from fibres of waste cotton materials shredded

Deflection Amount of movement from level of upholstery suspension system

Diamond buttoning Insertion of covered buttons into upholstery to form diamond shapes with pleating

Doming Amount of rise in centre of seat or cushion

Dowelled joint Timber joint held together with wooden pegs and glue

Down Fine fluffy covering on underside of waterfowl used for cushion and pillow filling

Feather Coarse covering of poultry and waterfowl. Generally containing thick quills

Fibre Coarse filling for first stuffing

Fibre fill Man-made fibres matted into thick soft layer form for use over foam interiors

Fine needle Long, slender, thin needle used for buttoning

Fine tacks Slender tacks with small diameter heads

First stuffing The initial layer of coarse filling in traditional upholstery

Flaxcord Best quality cord used to lash springs

Flys Strips of hessian sewn to edges of covering for economy purposes

Fullness Surplus covering causing unsightly wrinkling

Full seat Fully upholstered seat needing no cushion

'G' cramp Small timber cramp in the form of a 'G'

Gimp   Narrow decorative band to hide tacks

Gimp pins   Fine small coloured tacks mainly used to fix gimp, also with other uses

Ground work   The initial stage in preparation for diamond buttoning

Gutter   A channel formed with hessian between edge and seat springs

Hemp cord   Cord used for spring lashing made from hemp fibres

Hessian   (Canvas) Coarse cloth made from jute fibre used to support upholstery filling

Hide pincers   Wide-jaw pincers for tensioning leather, may also be used for webbing

Hoghair   Short stranded filling for upholstery filling

Horsehair   Good quality long stranded curled filling for upholstery

Improved tacks   Tacks with thicker shanks and wider heads than fine tacks

Laidcord   Cord for lashing springs. Cord fibres are laid parallel

Lashing   Tying of springs to prevent lateral movement

Latex foam   Upholstery foam made from sap of the rubber tree

Leather   Upholstery covering usually cow hide

Linen webbing   Good quality webbing woven from flax and cotton fibres

Lip   Front section of seat with cushion over

Mitre join   Diagonal join in fabric

Mortice   Section of timber joint into which a tenon fits

Occasional chair   A chair of light construction which may be used under varying circumstances

Pincore foam   Latex foam moulded with fine pin holes through its thickness

Piping Form of decoration to hide and strengthen seams in cushions, *etc*

Platform Rear section of seat with cushion over

Polyether/polyurethane foam Upholstery foam produced by mixture of chemicals

Rasp Coarse wood file

Rebate Recess machined in timber frame for tacking of covering

Regulator An upholsterer's needle with a 'flat' at one end

Resilient rubber webbing Webbing made from rubber with interlays of rayon cords to prevent over-stretching

Ripping chisel Blunt-bladed tool for removing tacks

Roll stitch A thick stitched upholstered edge

Ruche A decorative trimming machined into cushion seams, *etc*

Sash cramp Bar with adjustable jaws for cramping timber joints

Scrim Fabric with open weave used to encase filling for stitching

Second stuffing Final layer of softer filling in traditional upholstery

Simulated leather Plastic-coated fabric with leather appearance

Sinuous spring (Serpentine) A wire spring length formed with a series of U bends

Skewers Long pins with looped end for temporary holding of materials

Spatular A flat broad instrument for spreading adhesive

Spoon back Upholstered back with concave surface

Spring needle A thick strong curved needle to sew springs to webbing, *etc*

Spring unit Assembly of coil springs within a wire framework

Stay rail   A thin construction rail at base of back or arm

Stile   A part of the construction of upholstery frame interfering with tuck through of covering

Stuffing ties   Line of twine ties running through scrim, stuffing and hessian

SWG   Standard wire gauge

Tack roll   A method of softening a rail around edge of seat, etc

Tack tiles   Lines showing across fabric caused by overstraining with tacks

Teased filling   Filling which has been opened or loosened with the fingers

Template   A paper or card shape used for accurate cutting of covering

Tenon   Section of timber joint fitting into a mortice slot

Tension spring   A small diameter elongated extension spring

Top stitch   Final row of stitching on stuffed and stitched seat to give a sharp edge

LIST OF SUPPLIERS

Aberkenfig Upholstery, 5 Bridgend Road, Aberkenfig, Bridgend, Glam

Acre Furnishing Services Ltd, 38–40 Kennington Park Road, London, SE11 4RS

Andrews Upholstery, 302 Oxford Road, Reading, Berks, RG3 1ER

Anglia Upholstery (Ipswich) Ltd, Unit 12, Dedham Place Workshop, Water Works Street, Ipswich, Suffolk

Antiques of Tomorrow, 17 Tower Street, Rye, East Sussex, TN31 7AU. (Polished and unpolished frames and velvet coverings only)

Aquarius Soft Furnishing, 5a Hamilton House, Heath Road, Cox Heath, Maidstone, Kent

A. Baker & Son, 71a Fore Street, Ipswich, Suffolk, IP4 1JZ

Barking Home Improvements, 350 Ripple Road, Barking, Essex

Barnes & Co (Materials), Kangley Bridge Road, Sydenham, London, SE26 5AX

Collins, 56 Chapel Street, Luton, Beds

Coventry Foam and Upholstery Supplies, 65–69 Coventry Street, Stoke, Coventry, CV2 4ND

Dee Cee, 27 Hayburn Road, Millbrook Estate, Southampton, Hants

Dudley Home Interiors, Vine House, Fair Green Reach, Cambridge

Mervyn Durant, 3 Frian Street, Bridgewater, Somerset

The Easy Chair, 30 Lyndhurst Road, Worthing, Sussex

R. Eldridge, 502 Portswood Road, Southampton, Hants, SO5 3SA

A. C. Fish, Bullace Lane, r/o 82 High Street, Dartford, Kent

Fringe & Fabrics, Station Road, Broxbourne, Herts

G.E.M. Upholstery, 157 Southend Road, Grays, Essex, RM17 5NP

Gravesham Upholstery, 4–5 East Milton Road, Gravesend, Kent

W. E. Harryman, 145 Half Moon Lane, Herne Hill, London, SE24 9JY

J. E. Janes, 32 Clarence Road, Grays, Essex, RM17 6QJ

Jonmar Upholstery, The Old Maltings, St. Andrews Street South, Bury St. Edmunds, Suffolk

K. & M. Upholstery, 165 Luckwell Road, Bristol, BS3 3HB

Morgan Handyman Supplies, 27 Carlton Road, Nottingham, Notts

N. R. Neve, 31 The Broadway, St. Ives, Hunts., PE17 4BX

A. C. Prickett & Sons Ltd, 42 The Broadway, Leigh-on-Sea, Essex

F. E. Puleston Co. Ltd, r/o 148 Leagrave Road, Luton, Beds

A. J. Roberts & Co Ltd, 8 Tudor Road, Cardiff, CF1 8RF

Russell Trading Co, 75 Paradise Street, Liverpool, L1 3BP

Mr. A. Smith, 5a High Street, Hadleigh, Suffolk

Strand Upholstery, 793 Southchurch Road, Southend-on-Sea, Essex

Superease Upholstery, 5 Hannah Street North, Rhondda, Glam

I. R. Taylor, 12 Malpas Road, Newport, Gwent, NPT 5PA

Theobald Upholstery, Unit 7, Lodge Road, Staplehurst, Kent

F. W. Tuck, Russells Yard, Bell Street, Great Baddow, Essex

Yeovil Upholsteries D.I.Y. Supply Centre, 9 Wyndham Street, Yeovil, Somerset

If you have difficulty in obtaining supplies, upon receipt of S.A.E. the following company will forward details of your nearest supplier and the sundries available:

D. L. Foster Ltd,
12 The Ongar R, 20 Ongar Road, Great Dunmow,
Essex CM6 1EU.

INDEX